Using Images to Teach Critical Thinking Skills

Recent Titles in the Tech Tools for Learning Series

The Networked Library: A Guide for the Educational Use of Social Networking Sites
Melissa A. Purcell

Bookmarking: Beyond the Basics
Alicia E. Vandenbroek

School Library Infographics: How to Create Them, Why to Use Them
Peggy Milam Creighton

3D Printing: A Powerful New Curriculum Tool for Your School Library
Lesley M. Cano

Multimedia Learning Stations: Facilitating Instruction, Strengthening the Research Process, Building Collaborative Partnerships
Jen Spisak

Using Images to Teach Critical Thinking Skills

Visual Literacy and Digital Photography

DIANE M. CORDELL

TECH TOOLS FOR LEARNING

JUDI REPMAN, SERIES EDITOR

LIBRARIES UNLIMITED™
An Imprint of ABC-CLIO, LLC
Santa Barbara, California • Denver, Colorado

Library of Congress Cataloging-in-Publication Data

Cordell, Diane.
  Using images to teach critical thinking skills : visual literacy and digital photography / Diane M. Cordell.
      pages cm. — (Tech tools for learning)
  Includes bibliographical references and index.
    ISBN 978-1-4408-3515-5 (paperback) – ISBN 978-1-4408-3516-2 (ebook)
1. Visual literacy. 2. Photography—Digital techniques 3. Photography in education. 4. Critical thinking—Study and teaching (Elementary)
5. Critical thinking—Study and teaching (Secondary) 6. School librarian participation in curriculum planning. I. Title.
  LB1068.C67 2016
    370.15'5—dc23   2015025221

ISBN: 978-1-4408-3515-5

EISBN: 978-1-4408-3516-2

20 19 18 17 16   1 2 3 4 5

This book is also available on the World Wide Web as an eBook.
Visit www.abc-clio.com for details.

Libraries Unlimited
An Imprint of ABC-CLIO, LLC

ABC-CLIO, LLC
130 Cremona Drive, P.O. Box 1911
Santa Barbara, California 93116-1911

This book is printed on acid-free paper ∞

Manufactured in the United States of America

To those I love:

Mom & Dad

Tim

Ellen & Sean, Scott & Jackie

and my darling Morgan

Contents

PART I: Visual Literacy

PART II: Photography

PART III: Digital Images in the Classroom

Introduction

"The human being, creature of eyes, needs the image."
—Leonardo da Vinci

Mankind has historically used images as a medium for communication, from the rock art painted in Spanish and French caves 30,000 years ago to the infographics and digital photos of our modern era.

Developmentally, humans begin receiving information via their eyes at birth, with the vision skill set continuing to develop and strengthen throughout the first few years of life. Long before a baby masters the spoken language, he or she is able to track objects, distinguish colors, and recognize faces. By the age of two, a toddler's interactions with his or her environment show evidence of hand-eye coordination and depth perception. Language and reading skills depend upon these foundation visual skills. According to optometrist and vision development and vision therapy specialist Mary McMains, "75–90% of learning in a classroom occurs through the visual system . . . 80% of what you perceive, comprehend and remember depends on the efficiency of the visual system" (2006, *Vision and Learning*).

Infants will spend much of their early months developing visual skills. "Playing." (Photo by the author, all rights reserved.)

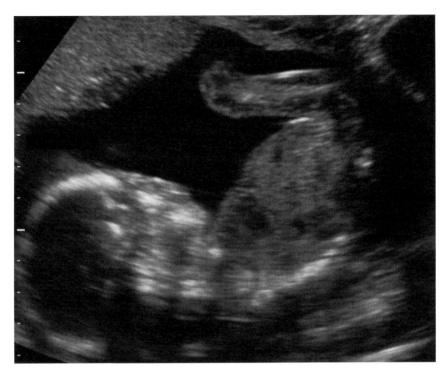

A person's digital footprint may begin building before birth. "Sonogram." (Photo by the author, all rights reserved.)

Photography is almost universally a part of contemporary life, and images comprise a significant portion of the digital footprint humans begin building at birth—or before. With the widespread use of mobile phones, most people carry a camera with them at all times. Apps linking to social networking sites allow for the seamless creation, editing, and sharing of images. The venerable *Oxford Dictionary* recognized the ubiquity of this practice by adding the word "selfie" ("a photograph that one has taken of oneself, typically one taken with a smartphone or webcam and uploaded to a social media website") to its lexicon as the 2013 International Word of the Year.

With the Maker movement gaining momentum, many people are turning to Pinterest, a virtual bulletin board, to search for crafting and creating ideas, as well as to YouTube for video tutorials. Finished products are showcased on Tumblr (a blogging platform and social networking site) or Flickr (image hosting website) and offered for sale on Etsy and eBay (global marketplaces), where photographs provide the sort of details about form, color, and condition that buyers look for when considering potential purchases.

In a school setting, makerspaces provide the opportunity for students to explore their passions and feel the satisfaction of creating an original product. For those who might not shine in traditional academic disciplines, having access to such an area could be the key to kindling an interest in education. Being a maker involves using a multitude of literacies in the search for inspiration. Makers are information consumers, and visual literacy is one of the skills that unlocks the information they need to be successful.

While studying online reading, the Transliteracies Project group, headed by Alan Liu, examined the interaction among literacies, specifically, text literacy,

For this "selfie," the author used the glass in a work-area door to take a self-portrait. "Spirit of the Library." (Photo by the author, Creative Commons license, some rights reserved. Retrieved from https://www.flickr.com/photos/dmcordell/3195847950.)

This high school student was quite knowledgeable about how to use—and disassemble for cleaning—a DSLR camera. "Student Photographer." (Photo by the author, Creative Commons license, some rights reserved. Retrieved from https://www.flickr.com/photos/dmcordell/16475943417.)

Students observe history in the making as they watch a live broadcast of President Barack Obama's January 2009 inaugural speech. "History Class: Presidential Inauguration." (Photo by the author, Creative Commons license, some rights reserved. Retrieved from https://www.flickr.com/photos/dmcordell/16495682970.)

Sometimes visual information is more useful than written directions. "At Time of Need." (Photo by the author, Creative Commons license, some rights reserved. Retrieved from http://flickr.com/photos/dmcordell/3596511470.)

visual literacy, and digital literacy. This group's working definition, a starting point for further research by Montfort University professor Sue Thomas and others, identified transliteracy as "the ability to read, write and interact across a range of platforms, tools and media from signing and orality through handwriting, print, TV, radio and films, to digital social networks" (2007, *Transliteracy: Crossing Divides*). Being literate in the 21 century, therefore, includes a range of competencies and skill sets, and visual literacy is an intrinsic part of the mix.

Another significant concept in contemporary education is "critical thinking," which emphasizes the need to objectively analyze and evaluate data. In an age of multimedia communication, proficiency in interpreting digital content, including digital images, is a necessary skill. The International Society for Technology in Education (ISTE) Standards for Students, American Association of School Librarians (AASL) Standards for the 21st-Century Learner, Association of College and Research Libraries (ACRL) Visual Literacy Competency Standards for Higher Education, and the Common Core State Standards (CCSS) Initiative all build upon the foundation concept of critical thinking.

Recognizing the highly visual nature of our society, the ACRL identified a need for specific standards addressing visual literacy. The Standards, Performance Indicators, and Learning Outcomes shared by this organization reflect this perspective. According to the CCSS website, "Across the English language arts and mathematics standards, skills critical to each content area are emphasized. In particular, problem-solving, collaboration, communication, and critical-thinking skills are interwoven into the standards" (Common Core FAQ). To meet these and similar standards, students are expected to process information from diverse sources and to demonstrate mastery by incorporating both print and nonprint resources when creating authentic products.

Melissa Thibault and David Walbert of the University of North Carolina at Chapel Hill identify an additional visual literacy skill, that of finding meaning in *visual relationships*: "The skills necessary to identify details of images are included in many disciplines; for example, careful observation is essential to scientific inquiry. But while accurate observation is important, *understanding* what we see and comprehending visual relationships is at least as important. These higher-level visual literacy skills require critical thinking, and they are essential to a student's success in any content area in which information is conveyed through visual formats" (2003, *Reading Images: An Introduction to Visual Literacy*).

If ours is an information age, then the analysis, evaluation, and synthesis of information, in whatever medium it is accessed, becomes a necessary competency, empowering learners to both discover and create knowledge. Increasingly, that information is being delivered as a visual resource.

Resource Box 1

Huffington Post, Brit Morin, "What Is the Maker Movement and Why Should You Care?" http://www.huffingtonpost.com/brit-morin/what-is-the-maker-movemen_b_3201977.html

Pinterest http://www.pinterest.com

YouTube http://www.youtube.com

Tumblr https://www.tumblr.com

Flickr https://www.flickr.com

Etsy http://www.etsy.com

eBay http://www.ebay.com

ISTE Standards for Students http://www.iste.org/docs/pdfs/20-14_ISTE_Standards-S_PDF.pdf

AASL Standards for the 21st-Century Learner http://www.ala.org/aasl/sites/ala.org.aasl/files/content/guidelinesandstandards/learningstandards/AASL_Learning Standards.pdf

ACRL Visual Literacy Competency Standards for Higher Education http://www.ala.org/acrl/standards/visualliteracy

Common Core State Standards Initiative http://www.corestandards.org

---

Organizational Note

Information in this book is shared in a variety of ways:

- **Text**

- **Images**—complement the written text, with **captions** to further clarify key concepts. All images include credits.

- **Resource boxes**—contain links to related websites mentioned in the text as well as additional relevant content.

- **Table of Contents**—a sequential listing of topics addressed.

- **Works Cited**—references used when composing the text.

- **Index**—alphabetical listing of key topics.

Part I

Visual Literacy

What Is Visual Literacy?

"Learn to see, and then you'll know there is no end to the new worlds of our vision."

—Carlos Castaneda

There are numerous definitions of visual literacy, from the very basic "Visual Literacy is the ability to read and write images" (Velders, De Vries, and Vaicaityte, 2007, *Visual Literacy and Visual Communication for Global Education*) to the more nuanced:

> Visual Literacy refers to a group of vision-competencies a human being can develop by seeing and at the same time having and integrating other sensory experiences. The development of these competencies is fundamental to normal human learning. When developed, they enable a visually literate person to discriminate and interpret the visible actions, objects, symbols, natural or man-made, that he encounters in his environment. Through the creative use of these competencies, he is able to communicate with others. Through the appreciative use of these competencies, he is able to comprehend and enjoy the masterworks of visual communication. (Debes, 1968, *What Is "Visual Literacy"?*)

Taking into account the revised Bloom's Taxonomy, a progressive hierarchy of desired learning outcomes, visual literacy might be expressed as "the ability to comprehend, analyze, evaluate, create, and communicate with, images."

Among the vision-competencies necessary for success in a literate society are eye-tracking skills (eyes following a line of print), eye-teaming skills (two eyes working together as a synchronized team), binocular vision (simultaneously blending the images from both eyes into one image), accommodation (eye focusing), visual-motor integration (eye-hand coordination), and visual perception (visual memory, visual form perception, and visualization). The fact that children lacking these skills are screened for both physical and cognitive problems points to how crucial the skill set is to normal growth and development.

In 1991, Howard Gardner identified seven distinct "intelligences," asserting that "The broad spectrum of students—and perhaps the society as a whole—would be better served if disciplines could be presented in a numbers of ways and learning could be assessed through a variety of means" (1991, p. 12). The multiple intelligences (MI) were designated visual-spatial, bodily-kinesthetic, musical, interpersonal, intrapersonal, linguistic, and logical-mathematical. An eighth intelligence, naturalistic (understanding the natural world of plants and animals, noticing their characteristics, and categorizing them),

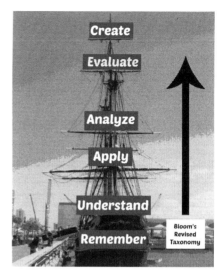

has since been added to the original seven. Teachers were urged to differentiate classroom instruction and assessment to accommodate the learning styles of their students by incorporating visuals, sound, movement, and other diverse elements in addition to written text.

A number of school districts base their curriculum on Gardner's MI theory. At the Gardner School of Arts and Sciences in Vancouver, Washington, "Howard Gardner's theory of multiple intelligences provides the framework for teaching and learning," with "teaching to the uniqueness of each individual" part of the school's Mission Statement. In its Approach to Learning Statement, New City School in St. Louis, Missouri, explains, "Our use of multiple intelligences theory as a basis for curriculum enhances the strength of our academic program. It allows children to develop in many different ways and to use their range of strengths and talents for learning and growing." Enota Multiple Intelligences Academy in Gainesville, Georgia, includes in its Core Beliefs, "Students learn and achieve success in different ways using their multiple intelligences."

While acknowledging the existence of learning style *preferences*, cognitive psychologists Cedar Riener and Daniel Willingham contend, "Students differ in their abilities, interests, and background knowledge, but not in their learning styles. Students may have preferences about how to learn, but no evidence suggests that catering to those preferences will lead to better learning. As college educators, we should apply this to the classroom by continuing to present information in the most appropriate manner for our content and for the level of prior knowledge, ability, and interests of that particular set of students" (2010, "The Myth of Learning Styles").

Riener and Willingham believe that a key concern in conveying information is selecting the modality that best suits the content. There are many instances when an image is the most appropriate choice to convey information, for example, when discussing constellations, describing nature trails, or identifying cloud

As with any other skill, visual literacy must be practiced and refined. "Gallery." (Photo by the author, Creative Commons license, some rights reserved. Retrieved from http://flickr.com/photos/dmcordell/15264187435.)

Even young children are capable of performing critical thinking tasks. A toddler was asked to choose magazine images that represent characteristics of her favorite toy ponies. "Baby's First Collage." (Photo by the author, Creative Commons license, some rights reserved. Retrieved from http://flickr.com/photos/dmcordell/14954435519.)

formations. Whether learners express a personal preference for visual, auditory, or kinesthetic experiences, they need to be critical consumers of data presented visually in our modern multimedia culture.

In a conversation with *Nieman Reports* editor Melissa Ludtke, Marcel Just, the director of the Center for Cognitive Brain Imaging at Carnegie Mellon University, discussed how the human brain processes information:

> Print isn't something the human brain was built for. The printed word is a human artifact. It's very convenient and it's worked very well for us for 5,000 years, but it's an invention of human beings. By contrast Mother Nature has built into our brain our ability to see the visual world and interpret it . . . you can circumvent written language to a large extent. A lot of printed words are there to describe things that occur spatially. In many cases a picture is worth a thousand words. Now we can generate these pictures and graphics and we can convey them to other people very easily. I think it's inevitable that visual media are going to become more important in conveying ideas. (2010, "Watching the Human Brain Process Information")

While Just does not believe that the written word is going to "go away," he anticipates an increasingly digital and visual mode of accessing data.

Visual literacy infuses all aspects of learning and is an integral part of every curricular area. From historic maps to star charts to geometry diagrams to primary source artifacts, images convey a vital flow of information requiring interpretation and assessment. Images enlighten and engage the learner, who must necessarily become adept at both using and doing, consuming and creating visual information.

Anne Bamford writes, "A visually literate person is able to discriminate and make sense of visual objects and images; create visuals; comprehend and appreciate the visuals created by others; and visualise objects in their mind's eye. To be an effective communicator in today's world, a person needs to be able to interpret, create and select images to convey a range of meanings" (2003, *The Visual Literacy White Paper*).

The formal teaching of visual literacy skills often stops once children learn to read and comprehend text. However, our students inhabit an information landscape in which visual data is a key component. In school, at work, and in everyday life, humans receive a steady stream of images:

photographs, infographics, maps, illustrations, advertisements, etc., which must be processed, interpreted, validated, and incorporated into their personal knowledge base. In the modern world, visual fluency is a critical literacy skill.

Resource Box 2

International Visual Literacy Association (IVLA) http://ivla.org/drupal2/content/what-visual-literacy

Gardner School of Arts and Sciences http://www.gardnerschool.org/programs/curriculum/multiple-intelligences

New City School http://www.newcityschool.org

Enota Multiple Intelligences Academy http://www2.gcssk12.net/schoolsites/eesweb/about-emia.html

---

Visual Literacy and Critical Thinking

"Criticism has hugely overestimated the centrality of language to Western culture. It has failed to see the electrifying sign language of images."

—Camille Paglia

ritical thinking emphasizes logical reasoning based on the judicious analysis of information. The critical thinker gathers data from a variety of sources, then interprets, evaluates, organizes, and reflects upon the accumulated evidence, ultimately using the knowledge gained to make decisions or create new products. In a school setting, student engagement is a key motivational factor in nurturing the inquiring mind-set. Images can supply both information and motivation, but, as with text, the images need to be vetted for accuracy, reliability, relevance, and timeliness. To be information literate, it is necessary to possess the critical thinking skill set. Both text and photographs must be regarded through a critical lens.

The Partnership for 21st Century Skills' P21 Common Core Toolkit points out in its Alignment Overview, "the CCSS [Common Core State Standards] documents establish critical thinking, reasoning, communication, and media/information/technology literacy in English Language Arts (ELA) and mathematics as key performance outcomes around which curricula and assessments should be focused" (2011). Critical thinking, communication, and collaboration are stressed in CCSS and other state and national compilations of student academic benchmarks. When writing its Declaration of Principles on Tolerance, UNESCO (United Nations Educational, Scientific and Cultural Organization) recognized

United Nations Educational, Scientific and Cultural Organization (UNESCO) promotes critical thinking and education for tolerance. (Photo by USAID_IMAGES, Creative Commons license, some rights reserved. Retrieved from http://flickr.com/photos/usaid_images/5012422171; some color adjustments made.)

the importance of critical thinking skills: "Education for tolerance should aim at countering influences that lead to fear and exclusion of others, and should help young people to develop capacities for independent judgment, critical thinking and ethical reasoning" (1995, Article 4.3).

In its online journal *Keeping Up With*, the Association of College and Research Libraries (ACRL) points out,

> visual literacy does not arise from sheer exposure to visual content. Students' ability to take photos, find images, and post visual content to online spaces does not automatically translate into the ability to critically engage with, make meaning from, and communicate with visual materials in an academic context. Images differ from texts in unique ways, and working with them effectively requires deliberate learning and practice. Students need opportunities to work thoughtfully with visual content so that they can learn to interpret, analyze, evaluate, and use images reflectively and ethically. (2011, *Keeping Up With . . . Visual Literacy*)

The enGauge report "Literacy in the Digital Age" lists visual literacy as one of the key skills for the future, identifying it as "the ability to interpret, use, appreciate, and create images and video using both conventional and 21st century media in ways that advance thinking, decision making, communication, and learning" (2003, p. 15).

Visual literacy involves making informed judgments, whether learners are selecting the best source to fulfill information needs or creating a unique product of their own. The photographer, for example, makes a series of design decisions about location, composition, lighting, color, and editing when capturing an image through the lens of a camera.

Another aspect of critical thinking that is becoming increasingly important in both education and the business world is curation. It is not enough to just gather resources, including images. The responsibilities of a curator include sorting through content, selecting the best offerings, arranging the chosen material in a meaningful and effective manner, and then publishing the collection for the use of a targeted audience. Well-curated collections are properly annotated and tagged, ensuring that they can be searched so that relevant items may be retrieved at time of need.

Critical thinking is necessary for intellectual growth. The skill sets developed through the practice of critical thinking can accomplish the following:

- help students determine the value of information accessed in all formats, including as digital images;

- guide choices regarding the creation of artifacts;

- influence the selection of where and how such artifacts might be shared ethically; and

- assist in the determination of which of the various curation options is best suited to preserve students' original visual products.

Critical thinking relies on reason rather than emotion. It is characterized by self-awareness, honesty, and open-mindedness. The critical thinker engages with, creates, and archives images in a mindful, reflective manner. He or she "sees" differently, questioning what is viewed with the understanding that meaning can be communicated in a variety of richly nuanced literacies.

Resource Box 3

P21 Common Core Toolkit http://www.p21.org/storage/documents/P21CommonCore Toolkit.pdf

Defining Critical Thinking http://www.criticalthinking.org/pages/defining-critical -thinking/766

Reading Digital Images

"The eye sees only what the mind is prepared to comprehend."
—Henri Bergson

L earning how to "read" digital images is a skill requiring guided practice. The process begins with a close examination of the image, identifying details that are of immediate interest as well as those that might bear further investigation. Guiding questions such as "What do you see?" "What does this remind you of?" "How does this make you feel?" and "What more would you like to know about this image?" help students examine their emotional and cognitive responses to what they are viewing and tap into their prior knowledge. As students gain expertise in visual literacy, they will be able to use critical thinking skills to provide evidence supporting their image analyses, offer critical evaluations, and create content modeled on what they have observed.

Part of the attraction of visuals is their immediacy. Advertisers understand this and use images as a visual hook to draw in consumers. However, reading images requires more than just comprehending what is instantly visible. The viewer must also use visual clues to determine the intentions of the image's creator by considering the social and historic context of the work. Information gained through the skilled reading of images serves to prove or disprove inferences made from an initial viewing and lead to truer understanding of what is seen.

There are a number of excellent, free resources that provide opportunities for teachers to engage students in the analysis of digital images.

The Library of Congress (LOC) website has numerous materials available for teachers and students relating to the use of primary source material. Primary Source Sets offer access to speeches, maps, photographs, cartoons, and videos on a wide range of topics, including the sport of baseball, the American Civil War, the Harlem Renaissance, and Found Poetry, just to name a few. The LOC's Primary Source Analysis Tool is a simple template that students can use to Observe, Reflect, Question, and note items for Further Investigation. Additional teacher guides offer strategies for facilitating student analysis of items from the Library's collection of Primary Sources, Oral Histories, Books, Photographs, Manuscripts, Political Cartoons, Maps, Sheet Music, Motion Pictures, and Sound Recordings, many of which are available online.

This primary-source photo shows a World War II soldier being trained for combat. "Ft. Eustis, VA July 1942." (Photo by author, Creative Commons license, some rights reserved. Retrieved from http://flickr.com/photos/dmcordell/14159572862.)

Also from the Library of Congress, the "Picturing Modern America 1880–1920" page features "Historic Thinking Exercises for Middle and High School Students." These activities utilize primary-source artifacts, particularly images, from the LOC's "American Memory" archives. "Image Detective" focuses on the close reading of photographs; "Investigations" invites students to interact with visual sources to track social change; and "Exhibit Builder" offers the opportunity to build a web-based historic collection by gathering and commenting upon images and documents. This last exercise incorporates research, reflection, and writing skills, and culminates with the creation of an authentic product that can be publicly shared.

Docs Teach, a site maintained by the National Archives, offers primary source material paired with critical thinking activities. Educators can access existing lessons linked to National History Standards, or create their own activities. The "Documents Analysis" page provides guidance on how to teach with documents (including images) in alignment with Bloom's Taxonomy.

Oakland Museum of California uses an interactive matching game to teach critical thinking skills. Players click on the photo of an artifact and then use visual clues to determine which of three images the object relates to. Links lead to further topical information about the history of the state of California.

What's going on in this picture? A child makes a keepsake rubbing of a soldier's name. "Vietnam Veterans Memorial: The Wall." (Photo by the author, Creative Commons license, some rights reserved. Retrieved from http://flickr.com/photos/dmcordell/13835921235.)

In October 2013, the *New York Times* began a new feature, "What's Going On in This Picture?" Each Monday, the newspaper posts a photo on its website that focuses on "*Times* photojournalism, visual literacy and critical thinking." The image initially has "no caption, no headline and no helpful link back to an article. To answer the question 'What's going on in this picture?' [students] have to rely solely on the information [they] can gather from the image itself—and from the online discussion with other students." Teachers are encouraged to ask three guiding questions: "What's going on in this picture?" "What do you see that makes you say that?" "What more can we find?" to stimulate classroom conversations and foster higher-thinking skills.

The critical thinker should have a clear understanding of what comprises valid sources and be able to judge which are best suited to specific information needs, regardless of format. He or she must be able to move beyond an initial response to an image and evaluate it objectively. As with most skills, proficiency in the decoding of visual images improves with practice.

*A Note about Visual Impairment

Graphicacy means the interpretation and creation of graphics. Visual impairment does not preclude the acquisition of this skill; modern technology offers tools to assist students in accessing and interpreting infographics and other images that they cannot see with their eyes.

Accessible designs include tactile copies, audio word descriptions, and audio-tactile graphics. The Seoul National School for the Blind used a 3-D printer to produce a "touchable yearbook," busts of graduating students modeled from photographs. Apps like TapTapSee, VizWiz, and Be My Eyes use the cameras on mobile devices to help users identify objects.

Resource Box 4

Library of Congress

- **Using Primary Sources** http://www.loc.gov/teachers/usingprimarysources
- **Primary Source Sets** http://www.loc.gov/teachers/classroommaterials/primary sourcesets
- **Primary Source Analysis Tool** http://www.loc.gov/teachers/primary-source-analysis -tool
- **Teacher Guides** http://www.loc.gov/teachers/usingprimarysources/guides.html
- **Historic Thinking Exercises for Middle and High School Students** http:// cct2.edc.org/PMA

National Archives

- **Docs Teach** http://docsteach.org
- **Find & Use Activities** http://docsteach.org/activities
- **Document Analysis with Students** http://docsteach.org/resources

Oakland Museum of California, Picture This http://www.museumca.org/picturethis/ match-objects

New York Times, **What's Going On in This Picture?** http://learning.blogs.nytimes .com/category/lesson-plans/whats-going-on-in-this-picture

The Touchable Yearbook http://distractify.com/pinar/3d-printed-touchable-yearbook

Tap Tap See http://www.taptapseeapp.com

VizWiz https://itunes.apple.com/US/app/id439686043?mt=8

Be My Eyes http://www.bemyeyes.org/

Tactile Picture Books Project http://www.tactilepicturebooks.org

Blind with Camera http://www.blindwithcamera.org

A team of academic researchers (professor and students) at the University of Colorado Boulder began the Tactile Picture Books Project to create 3-D versions of well-known children's stories. Even if there are no visually impaired students in your school, show sighted students photos of the project's adaptations and have them compare the tactile version to the original books. Ask students what was changed and why they think the alteration (or omission) was made. If there is a 3D printer available, challenge students to create artifacts that could be incorporated into a similar tactile book. Modify a picture walk by having students describe what they see to a classmate with visual limitations. Raise student awareness by showing them the site hosted by the Beyond Sight Foundation: Blind with Camera "provides a platform for the visually impaired to share their 'Inner Gallery' of images—their imagination and point-of-view of the visual world, and speak out about their unique experience, feelings, challenges and hopes." Initiate a discussion of what it means to see differently and how it might affect daily life.

Part II

Photography

A (Very) Brief History

"I have seized the light. I have arrested its flight."

—Louis Daguerre

Images are everywhere. In the course of a day, visual information is presented to us via news outlets, social networking sites, periodicals, television programs, video clips, and movies, on devices of all shapes and sizes.

Hunter Schwarz, of Buzzfeed, shares some amazing data: "Using film industry statistics, digital photography estimates and numbers kept by producers of silver halide, an important chemical for analog film, researchers calculated the number of photographs ever taken [to be] . . . 3.8 trillion photos . . . About ten percent of the photos ever taken have been taken in the past 12 months" (*How Many Photos Have Been Taken Ever?*, 2012).

First used by scientist Sir John F. W. Herschel in 1839, the word "photography" is derived from the Greek words *photos* (light) and *graphein* (to draw), but the idea of recording images from life is much older. Ancient Chinese and Greek philosophers understood the concept of the pinhole camera—the "camera obscura"—which projects an upside-down image of its surroundings on a screen for viewing or tracing. In 1800, Thomas Wedgwood attempted to capture such images permanently on material coated with light-sensitive chemicals.

Modern photography began in 1839, when Louis Daguerre introduced his daguerreotype process to the French Académie des Sciences. Daguerre promoted his invention, which recorded an image on a highly polished, silver-plated sheet of copper, as both artistic (portraits, landscapes) and scientific (fossils, animal specimens). He is generally credited as being one of the so-called Fathers of Photography. Within 40 years, American George Eastman had developed a dry-gel-on-paper product, or "film," to replace heavy photographic plates. Eastman's Brownie camera went into mass production in 1901, making photography accessible to the general public.

Early photographic images were black and white, sometimes tinted by hand. Based on prior investigations by Scottish physicist James Clerk Maxwell in 1855, Thomas Sutton produced color separations to use for an 1861 Maxwell lecture on physics. Further refinements by Louis Ducos du Hauron (1868), Hermann Wilhelm Vogel (1873), Edmond Becquerel (1874), and many others led to Kodak's introduction of Kodachrome tri-pack color in 1935. By the mid-1930s, home movies and slides could be taken in color. Color still prints became available in 1941.

Digital camera technology evolved from the same technology used for television images. Eastman Kodak engineer Steve Sasson built the first digital camera in 1975. It weighed 8 pounds and used a TV set to play back data recorded on cassette tapes. Commercially produced digital cameras, which downloaded to home computers, were initially sold in 1990, with improvements coming in succeeding years. The 1994 Olympus Deltis VC-1100 could transmit

The "camera obscura" was an optical device that helped inspire early photography devices. "Camera Obscura Box 18th Century," 19th-century dictionary illustration. (Unknown illustrator, licensed under public domain via Wikimedia Commons. Retrieved from http://commons.wikimedia.org/wiki/File:Camera_Obscura_box18thCentury.jpg#/media/File:Camera_Obscura_box-18thCentury.jpg.)

images over a phone line without needing a computer or other device; the following year, the Casio QV-10 offered a 1.8-inch color LCD (liquid crystal display screen) that could play back images and function as a viewfinder. Innovations by Sony, Nikon, Fujifilm, Canon, Minolta, and other companies led to the streamlined point-and-shoot and the more sophisticated DSLR (digital single-lens reflex) and mirrorless cameras of today.

Since digital cameras use memory cards in place of film, customers were freed from reliance on professional film labs to process their photographs. Seeing an opportunity for new markets, Kinko's and Microsoft collaborated with Kodak to introduce self-service store kiosks where customers could produce photo CDs or printouts. A variety of home printing options soon made the process even easier. Today, many digital camera users choose to simply upload, store, and display their images online on sites like Flickr, Picasa, Shutterfly, and Snapfish without resorting to print options at all. Others upload photos to commercial websites that offer such options as photos on canvas, printed books, or items customized with personal images. Digital cameras are now built into personal computing devices and smartphones. It is possible to take, edit, and share photographs almost instantly—and in quantities limited only by battery life and memory capacity.

Customers now have the option of uploading and printing their own photos on devices like this, found in many big box stores. "Self-Service." (Photo by the author, Creative Commons license, some rights reserved. Retrieved from http://flickr.com/photos/dmcordell/14169932602.)

Photographs have been part of the school experience for decades. An online search will return hundreds of primary source images of 19th- and 20th-century students, posed with their teachers, either inside a classroom or in front of their schoolhouse. Although earlier examples exist, yearbooks became more widely affordable in 1880, when letterpress process and halftone printing made it possible to mass produce such albums. School yearbooks are now, of course, a common practice, even for students in an elementary setting.

In the pre-digital era, taking and printing photographs was a fairly expensive proposition. Generally, the only people using cameras during the school day were yearbook staff or professional photographers on site for a planned photo session. When digital cameras first became widely available, some districts purchased one or two and added them to their library's media collection for use by administrators, teachers, and those students who had obtained special permission to borrow a camera to use for a project. Bringing devices to school from home was not a generally accepted practice.

Today, digital cameras are quite affordable. Some companies market simple designs intended for children as young as three years old. In addition, mobile phones and tablets capture images of surprisingly good quality. A popular and accessible activity, photography can be used in the classroom to generate interest, stimulate critical thinking, and provide opportunities for improving digital and visual literacy skills. Lessons planned to incorporate photography usually prove to be engaging and very popular with students.

Resource Box 5

Flickr https://www.flickr.com

Picasa http://picasa.google.com

Shutterfly http://www.shutterfly.com

Snapfish http://www.snapfish.com

Common Terms Used in Photography

"The limits of my language mean the limits of my world."
—Ludwig Wittgenstein

While it is not necessary to be an expert, understanding the basic vocabulary of photography will help even casual users become more proficient at making and interpreting digital images. The following list should provide a fairly comprehensive overview.

Ambient lighting: the natural or environment light present in a scene without additional flash or reflectors.

Aperture: the opening in a photographic lens that admits the light. The size of the opening is measured in numbers called f-stops, which are adjusted automatically or manually, depending on the type of camera being used.

App (application): a software program designed to perform a specific task, usually downloaded to a mobile device.

Autofocus: sensors in the camera lens automatically determine the correct focus for a sharp image; with a **manual focus**, the photographer must adjust settings for each shot by hand. Some cameras offer both options.

Bokeh: derived from the Japanese word *boke* ("blur" or "haze"), this term is used to describe an artistic blurring of an image background, usually seen as spots of light.

There is "bokeh" blurring in both the foreground and background of this image of a leaf. "Grape Leaf, Autumn." (Photo by the author, Creative Commons license, some rights reserved. Retrieved from http://flickr.com/photos/dmcordell/10731663313.)

A collage can be used to display themed photos in a pleasing arrangement. "Monterey Collage." (Photo by the author, Creative Commons license, some rights reserved. Retrieved from https://www.flickr.com/photos/dmcordell/16060799384.)

Collage: multiple images combined into a single image. Most editing sites offer a variety of collage options.

Color balance: the accuracy with which the colors captured in the image match the original scene.

Colorize: to add color to a black and white photo using computer technology.

Composition: how different design elements (positioning, lighting, framing, mood, color, etc.) work together to produce an effective image.

Extreme cropping can cause a photo to lose much of its detail. A telephoto lens or zoom option would be a better choice here. "Scaffold." (Photo by the author, Creative Commons license, some rights reserved. Retrieved from https://www.flickr.com/photos/dmcordell/16497094179.)

An extended depth of field draws the viewer's eyes into this photo of a garden. "Plains of Abraham, Joan of Arc Garden." (Photo by the author, Creative Commons license, some rights reserved. Retrieved from http://flickr.com/photos/dmcordell/7877238480.)

A shallow depth of field directs the viewer's attention to the main subject of interest in this image. "To Violets." (Photo by the author, Creative Commons license, some rights reserved. Retrieved from http://flickr.com/photos/dmcordell/14098848664.)

A drone with a camera attached can capture stunning aerial views. "Drone and Moon." (Photo by Don McCullough, Creative Commons license, some rights reserved. Retrieved from http://flickr.com/photos/69214385@N04/8725078749.)

Overexposed images can be adjusted during the editing process. "Window." (Photo by the author, Creative Commons license, some rights reserved. Retrieved from http://flickr.com/photos/dmcordell/16213489343.)

Cropping: trimming the size of an image. While this will enlarge a specific portion of an image, some detail may be lost when the photo is cropped.

Depth of field: the area of an image that is in focus.

Download: transfer an image from a camera to a computer.

Drone: an unmanned aerial vehicle (UAV). These remotely piloted small aircraft can be fitted with cameras and used to take aerial photographs.

DSLR: a digital single-lens reflex camera. This type of camera has interchangeable lenses and can be focused automatically or manually. Because

GoPro cameras can be fastened to a chest strap or helmet to capture action shots. "Through the Eyes of a Paratrooper: 173rd Jumps in Ukraine for Rapid Trident 2011," (Photo by U.S. Army Europe Images, Creative Commons license, some rights reserved. Retrieved from http://flickr.com/photos/usarmyeurope_images/5979156687; image has been resized.)

of larger image sensors, DSLRs produce a higher image quality than do the simpler point-and-shoot cameras.

Editing: altering an image. This might entail cropping, color or exposure adjustment, or a variety of special effects.

Exposure: the amount of light reaching a camera's sensor. Improperly exposed photos can be adjusted, to some extent, during editing.

Field of view: that part of the world seen in an image; the area of coverage.

Filter: a glass screen that fits over a lens and controls color or light intensity.

Focus: (n.) the distinctness of an image; (v.) to adjust a camera to produce a clear image.

GoPro: a durable type of camera, often used for extreme action shots, that can be worn or mounted on a vehicle, including a drone.

JPEG (.jpg): a method of compressing images so that they can be stored and transmitted on the Internet.

Landscape: a scene rather than a single object.

Landscape mode: when you hold the camera in its normal horizontal position to take a photo.

For **portrait mode,** you rotate the camera to capture an image with a vertical orientation.

Sometimes a city landscape can be just as effective as a rural one. "Chicago River." (Photo by the author, Creative Commons license, some rights reserved. Retrieved from http://flickr.com/photos/dmcordell/9202268401.)

Layering: editing only one area of a photograph, without affecting its other parts. Also used to refer to the process of stacking one image on top of another.

Here a photographer has skillfully layered a shot of the moon with the image of a stork on its nest. "I Can't Get No Sleep." (Photo by Feliciano Guimarães, Creative Commons license, some rights reserved. Retrieved from http://flickr.com/photos/jsome1/3422512294.)

LCD: liquid-crystal display, the technology embedded in the back of digital cameras, providing a screen that serves both as a viewfinder when taking a photograph and as a review mechanism after taking a photograph. Some cameras have a separate, dedicated viewfinder as well.

Lens: the part of the camera through which light enters.

Macro: an extreme close-up of an object. Most cameras have a macro setting; more powerful macro lenses are available for cameras with interchangeable lenses.

Memory card: a small, flat flash drive that stores digital information on a camera. This is the equivalent of film in a digital camera. Once the images are downloaded, the card can be reused again and again. Some photographers buy extra memory cards to take along on outings when they expect to take a very large number of pictures.

Mirrorless camera: a mirrorless interchangeable-lens camera (MILC) does not have a mirror reflex optical viewfinder. These cameras take high-quality pictures but can weigh considerably less than a comparable DSLR model.

Panorama: "stitching together" a series of photos to create a wider-than-normal image. Panoramic views can be made by employing editing software to combine successive images or by using apps available for mobile devices.

"Macro" images can reveal unexpected beauty in the natural world. This photo shows the delicate loveliness of a single snowflake. "Snowfall." (Photo by the author, Creative Commons license, some rights reserved. Retrieved from http://flickr.com/photos/dmcordell/11439793026.)

A panoramic or "pano" shot captures images with elongated fields of view. It is also known as wide format photography. "Bolton Landing, Lake George, NY." (Photo by the author, Creative Commons license, some rights reserved. Retrieved from https://www.flickr.com/photos/dmcordell/16681742181.)

Pic/Pix: common abbreviations for "picture" and "pictures."

Pixels: tiny picture elements (dots, squares, or rectangles) that the human eye blends naturally to form an image. The higher the number of pixels, the sharper an image will appear.

Point-and-shoot: a camera that automatically adjusts light and focus when its release button is pressed. This type of camera has a fixed lens and is more compact, and usually less costly, than a DSLR (digital single-lens reflex camera).

Portrait: the likeness of a person.

Tripods keep a camera steady. They are especially useful for long exposures. "Tripod." (Photo by the author, Creative Commons license, some rights reserved. Retrieved from https://www.flickr.com/photos/dmcordell/16497075819.)

Red-eye: the appearance of a person's eyes as red in a photograph. This is caused by a reflection of the camera flash in the retina of the eye. Red-eye can usually be corrected by editing.

Resolution: the sharpness and clarity of an image, determined by the number of pixels it contains.

Self-portrait: a representation of a person taken by him/herself. A **selfie** is a self-portrait typically taken with a mobile device and shared with others via a social networking site.

Tagging: adding keywords to images to make the image searchable. Tags can be used to identify the people, the location, or the event shown in a picture.

Tripod: an adjustable three-legged stand used to steady a camera.

Vignette: when the edges of an image are either darkened or lightened in relation to the rest of the photo. It has the effect of drawing the viewer into the photo. Many online editing sites offer a vignette effect.

Zoom: Using a camera lens to change the apparent distance of a subject. **Optical zoom** uses the optics (lens) of a camera to bring an object closer. **Digital zoom** automatically crops the image, resulting in a loss of resolution. For high-quality photographs, experts recommend choosing a device with optical zoom when purchasing a camera. Owners of cameras with interchangeable lenses have the option of using a **telephoto lens** for high-quality images of distant objects.

A telephoto lens makes it possible to take close-up wildlife photos. "The Lynx." (Photo by the author, Creative Commons license, some rights reserved. Retrieved from http://flickr.com/photos/dmcordell/8798997693.)

Some Principles of Design

"To design is to communicate clearly by whatever means you can control or master."

—Milton Glaser

In photography, as in any visual art, there are certain principles that, when followed, produce a more effective image.

Balance is the consideration of visual weight and importance. A photographer might decide upon a *symmetric* (formal balance) arrangement of objects, giving each side of the composition equal weight, with one side almost mirroring the other. Another option is *asymmetry* (informal balance), wherein both sides of the photo have equal weight but do not mirror each other. The asymmetric image is considered to produce more "movement," as the eye travels over the disparate elements.

An image without **contrast** tends to be bland and uninteresting. The lightness and darkness of a photograph can be controlled in a number of ways: through camera settings, filters, and positioning of the subject to create shadows or silhouettes. Editing tools also offer options for adjusting exposure and color.

The principle of **movement** means the viewer's eye is directed to various areas of the image rather than remaining fixed on a single element. One way to achieve this effect is through rhythm, the repetition of a **pattern**. Visually, this might translate into a single element or into a group of related objects that are repeated in a single image. A *regular rhythm*, with evenly spaced subjects, creates low energy; an *irregular rhythm*, with an intentional "interruption"

Both sides of this symmetric image have equal weight as they balance the central object. "Feather." (Photo by the author, Creative Commons license, some rights reserved. Retrieved from http://flickr.com/photos/dmcordell/8504359779.)

The dark "bones" of this abandoned barn contrast with a bright autumn day. "Skeleton." (Photo by the author, Creative Commons license, some rights reserved. Retrieved from http://flickr.com/photos/dmcordell/5086967528.)

An asymmetric off-centering of the main object creates interest and movement. "Pilot Boat." (Photo by the author, Creative Commons license, some rights reserved. Retrieved from http://flickr.com/photos/dmcordell/14184008766.)

included, generates higher energy. Both types of rhythm add interest to images. Movement is also generated through color, line, and shape choices.

By using **emphasis**, the creator of an image conveys the central message of the work. Placement, color, background, and contrast all serve to draw the viewer's eye to the key component, or **focal point**. While the subject of a photograph

A variation in the pattern of these flower petals adds interest to a nature shot. "The Sunflowers." (Photo by the author, Creative Commons license, some rights reserved. Retrieved from http://flickr.com/photos/dmcordell/9576972641.)

A blurred background and large shadowed area mean that the viewer's eye is drawn to a delicate, rain-dotted spiderweb in the foreground of the photo. "Web." (Photo by the author, Creative Commons license, some rights reserved. Retrieved from http://flickr. com/photos/dmcordell/15110733799.)

The angle from which the photo was taken makes a grasshopper appear much larger than its actual size. "The Giant." (Photo by the author, Creative Commons license, some rights reserved. Retrieved from http://flickr.com/photos/dmcordell/9861672804.)

is central to its message, it is also important to consider **negative space**, the area that allows the eye to "rest" from the central object. Negative space can be any color; it just does not have content that attracts attention.

Proportion is created when the size and scale of objects in the image retain their normal ratio. Deliberately distorting proportion—by shifting the angle of a shot or using specialty lenses—can create interest and tension.

The final principle of design, **unity** refers to the creation of a harmonious whole, which makes the finished product seem cohesive and complete. When all the elements in a work look as though they belong together, the artist has achieved unity.

There are some **composition techniques** that contribute to the unity of an image. **Rule of thirds** refers to the balance achieved by dividing a visual image into an imaginary grid, using two horizontal and two vertical lines to create nine equal parts. The horizon is placed on the bottom or the top line to avoid the appearance of cutting the photo in half. When the subject of a photograph is a person, the idea is to line up the body with a vertical line and the eyes with a horizontal line, having the majority of "open space" located in the direction toward which the subject is moving. Online editing sites such as PicMonkey and Ribbet automatically place a rule-of-thirds grid over images as part of their cropping tool.

"Rule of Thirds." (Photo by the author, Creative Commons license, some rights reserved. Retrieved from http://flickr.com/photos/dmcordell/1402660370.)

Movement as a composition technique can be created in a number of ways. Variation in the size and location of similar objects draws a viewer's eyes into the image. Blurring in a photo can suggest motion. Rather than a "mistake," many photographers seek to create blur as a desirable feature. Although professionals use a tripod for long exposures, it is possible to achieve the same effect with a point-and-shoot by holding the camera as still as possible, placing it on a stable object, or even bracing it against your body.

Another consideration when preparing to capture an image is **framing**. Paintings and photographs are put into frames to give them importance and to add to their visual appeal. While it is possible to add a variety of frames when editing—from museum frames with matting to faux photo edging to holiday borders—the photographer should also make use of natural frames. Tree branches, rock formations, and doorways all offer an easy way to give an image definition and create a sense of depth. What matters is that the framing element draws attention to the actual subject of the photo. Having subjects pose while holding up an actual frame or photo mat is becoming a popular event activity.

In addition to these principles of design, it is also important to keep in mind the six elements of art—line, shape, form, color, texture, and space—when analyzing or creating images. Successful photographs incorporate these elements, as do all of the visual arts. For example, while a digital image may be two-dimensional, proper use of lighting and color can convey the "feel" of a textured surface. Similarly, a photographer's use of

The blur in this image helps convey a feeling of joyous motion. "Twirling Princess." (Photo by the author, Creative Commons license, some rights reserved. Retrieved from http://flickr.com/photos/dmcordell/3388630818.)

Bare branches frame a bright-red barn in this winter landscape. "View from the Covered Bridge." (Photo by the author, Creative Commons license, some rights reserved. Retrieved from http://flickr.com/photos/dmcordell/6853285637.)

Decorative house trim frames the view of a city neighborhood. "View from the Top." (Photo by the author, Creative Commons license, some rights reserved. Retrieved from http://flickr.com/photos/dmcordell/8468836533.)

space, both positive and negative, can create the illusion of depth, drawing a viewer into the image. Deciding whether an image will be in color or black and white means choosing to emphasize line, shape, and form in distinctly different ways. Harmony, variety, proportion, balance, and contrast all enter into the composition of visually pleasing images.

Practical Tips for Effective Photography

"You don't make a photograph just with a camera. You bring to the act of photography all the pictures you have seen, the books you have read, the music you have heard, the people you have loved."

—Ansel Adams

When a child begins kindergarten, he or she most likely has already been the subject of numerous photographs taken by family and friends: slices of life that are shared and saved. Wedding photos, formal portraits, albums documenting parties and trips all become part of family and personal history. In addition to being pervasive in our society, photography is a very accessible art. Both the teacher, hoping to create visual content, and the student, enjoying the process of creating a pleasing product, can improve their skills with a bit of practice. Once the basics are mastered, photography can become a satisfying avocation and a lifelong passion.

The preceding section explained elements of good design. The following are some suggestions aimed at helping the novice photographer—of any age—take more interesting photos.

Know your camera. Before beginning any project, it is necessary to become familiar with your device. This is especially important in a school setting, if students will be expected to use borrowed equipment. Even point-and-shoot cameras have setting choices, so find and explain macro (extreme close-up setting, usually designated by a small flower icon), flash, nighttime, and similar options. Have each person practice using the on/off and zoom buttons. Discuss battery life and recharging; older students should also be able to locate the camera's memory card and battery. Tablets and smartphones are relatively simple to operate, but trying out the camera, and approved apps, ahead of time will help minimize problems and frustration once the photo activity begins. This introductory phase also offers

The arrows point to the macro flower icon on this point-and-shoot camera. "Macro." (Photo by the author, Creative Commons license, some rights reserved. Retrieved from http://flickr.com/photos/dmcordell/14269147226.)

Digital cameras are limited only by their battery life. Photograph the subject from a variety of angles and make a final selection during editing. "Take Lots of Shots." (Photo by the author, Creative Commons license, some rights reserved. Retrieved from http://flickr.com/photos/dmcordell/16832317192.)

the perfect opportunity to hone research skills. Many camera manuals, how-to guides, and step-by-step instructions can be found online. Let students become experts on their own devices and act as peer tutors for others in their class.

Be ready. Make sure all devices are charged before beginning. Nothing is more frustrating than being unable to take the "perfect" shot because a camera battery dies. Also, repeat instructions so that students have a clear understanding of what images they are expected to produce for an activity. Providing a checklist is another way to help students stay focused on a theme for the images they are making.

Take lots of shots. Freedom from film means an almost unlimited capacity for taking photos (subject to battery life and memory size). For photographers, more is always better; critical judgment can be exercised during the editing and curating phases. Access to a large number of raw images also offers the possibility of utilizing "mistake" shots, like blurred motion or bright bokeh, which can be quite effective as well.

Check immediately. It's important to review images periodically to be sure that they aren't consistently blurry or poorly centered. Macro shots can be especially challenging, since the lens will often focus on background details rather than the

When the camera lens in macro mode focuses on background details, rather than the main subject, a slight shift in angle might solve the problem. "Macro Focus." (Photo by the author, Creative Commons license, some rights reserved. Retrieved from http://flickr.com/photos/dmcordell/14294267564.)

intended subject. Slightly changing the angle of the camera or backing up a step or two can help remedy this issue. While editing can fix some problems, well-composed, properly focused images result in much more pleasing final products.

Provide stability. Look for ways to steady the camera: become a "human tripod" by holding elbows tight against the body. Rest devices on a flat surface, like a table, fence post, or railing when taking photos. While some experimental movies feature a "shaky cam" technique, most digital images look better when the camera is held firmly. Acquiring an inexpensive tripod might be a good idea if students will be taking nighttime or other shots that require longer exposure.

Move closer. It is easy to crop images while editing in order to enlarge the main subject; however, extensive cropping results in loss of detail. A better idea is to just reduce the distance between the camera and the object the photographer is trying to capture. Crouching or squatting, even lying down on the ground, might also be advisable in some instances, for example, when capturing nature macros. At other times, the use of a zoom lens may be more appropriate.

Choose interesting angles. Provide variety by shooting from different perspectives. Approach the object or scene from a number of directions. Although the subject may be still, the photographer should be in motion.

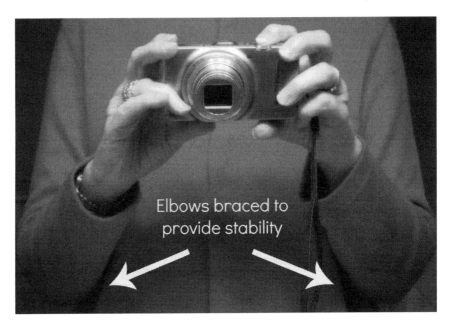

Elbows braced to provide stability

Holding the camera as still as possible helps prevent "shaky" images. "Braced." (Photo by the author, Creative Commons license, some rights reserved. Retrieved from http://flickr.com/photos/dmcordell/14307087835.)

Unusual angles result in more interesting images. "Flowers." (Photo by the author, Creative Commons license, some rights reserved. Retrieved from http://flickr.com/photos/dmcordell/13832123454.)

This photo of a paper birch tree zeroes in on its distinctive bark. "To Love What Is Mortal." (Photo by the author, Creative Commons license, some rights reserved. Retrieved from http://flickr.com/photos/dmcordell/8040051189.)

Focus on the detail. Not all subjects need to be perfectly centered and photographed in their entirety. Portraying the essence of an object by spotlighting a key attribute requires some higher-level thinking skills and creativity.

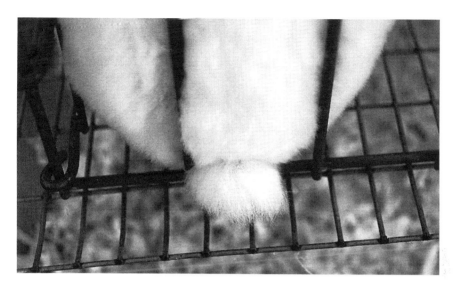

It is possible to identify this animal by a close-up shot of its fluffy tail, poking out of a cage at the county fair. "A Short Tale." (Photo by the author, Creative Commons license, some rights reserved. Retrieved from http://flickr.com/photos/dmcordell/4813389616.)

Palm-tree fronds form an interesting pattern when observed from the ground gazing up. "Palms." (Photo by the author, Creative Commons license, some rights reserved. Retrieved from http://flickr.com/photos/dmcordell/7475194346.)

Look up, look down, look back, look more closely. It is important to inject some variety into photos. Try to capture something engaging or unusual: the underside of a mushroom, tracks in the snow, the hidden heart of a flower. Find beauty in the ordinary.

Although this little frog makes a lot of noise, you need sharp eyes to spot him. "Hiding in Plain Sight." (Photo by the author, Creative Commons license, some rights reserved. Retrieved from http://flickr.com/photos/dmcordell/14133543149.)

Sometimes mundane creatures are fascinating if examined more carefully. "Inch by Inch." (Photo by the author, Creative Commons license, some rights reserved. Retrieved from http://flickr.com/photos/dmcordell/5151679089.)

Understand lighting. The direction of a light source, natural or artificial, and the shadows it creates will affect how the subject will appear. Front lighting minimizes texture and details; any shadows are behind the subject. Photos taken with a flash are front lit. Backlighting highlights shapes and casts strong shadows. With fewer details visible, side lighting captures contours and textures, producing more dramatic images. When a light source is diffused, either naturally (by clouds and fog, for example) or through the use of fabrics like muslin or silk, the light is softened and shadows are minimized. Diffused light is flattering for portraits but does not work as well with landscapes, where shadows lend interest.

Play with reflections. The selfie taken in a bathroom mirror is standard fare on social networking sites. Try taking advantage of other reflective surfaces—water, windows, polished metal—to record a self-portrait. Be aware that, if a flash is needed, the photographer should angle the shot to avoid a bright spot. If natural light seems sufficient, turn off the automatic flash for a few of the photos. Reflections also offer an opportunity to alter reality in unusual, creative ways, adding an abstract, artistic quality to photographs.

Tell a story. Stories are not just found in works of fiction. People tell stories to make sense of their world, and photographs can provide the visual "language" to help them do so. Capturing images is only the beginning; selecting and arranging them in a coherent narrative requires judgment and creativity. A single photograph might become the story starter for an English Language Arts composition activity, as writers consider "What if . . ." or "What comes next . . ." or other open-ended questions.

Always have a camera nearby, even if it's your smartphone. Life can present unexpected photo ops. While it's sometimes better to just stop and enjoy the moment, there will be images you long to capture and preserve. Be ready with some type of device handy. With the increasing sophistication of phone cameras, and the ease with which they can instantly edit and

This image of a marble column lacks depth of detail due to front lighting. "Ars Poetica." (Photo by the author, Creative Commons license, some rights reserved. Retrieved from http://flickr.com/photos/dmcordell/8656414098.)

The morning sun is behind these pines, resulting in silhouetted forms outlined by the burst of light. "There Is a Crack in Everything." (Photo by the author, Creative Commons license, some rights reserved. Retrieved from http://flickr.com/photos/dmcordell/9736748802.)

Side-lit images are even more dramatic in black and white. "Wings." (Photo by the author, Creative Commons license, some rights reserved. Retrieved from http://flickr.com/photos/dmcordell/8963961046.)

Clouds diffuse the light and soften objects in this winter photo. "New Year's Day, Lake George, NY." (Photo by the author, Creative Commons license, some rights reserved. Retrieved from http://flickr.com/photos/dmcordell/4234769076.)

Affectionately known as "The Bean," this stainless steel sculpture is a popular spot for taking selfies in Chicago. "Self-Portrait in the Cloud Gate." (Photo by the author, Creative Commons license, some rights reserved. Retrieved from http://flickr.com/photos/dmcordell/9202007057.)

share images, mobile phones are becoming the primary camera used by younger photographers.

Study the work of other photographers, both amateur and professional. Enhance your skills and sharpen your eyes by visiting photography exhibitions

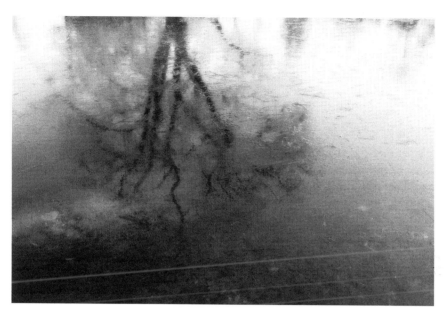

A partially frozen pond offers an artistic "interpretation" of a tree. "Icy Reflection." (Photo by the author, Creative Commons license, some rights reserved. Retrieved from http://flickr.com/photos/dmcordell/8197019133.)

at local galleries and museums. View the Explore page of Flickr, National Geographic's Photo of the Day, online resources from the National Gallery of Art, and similar websites. Learn from excellence but continue to develop and stay true to your personal artistic vision.

Back up your photographs. Save a set on your computer with additional copies off-line on a DVD, memory stick, or external hard drive. Even seemingly stable online photo storage sites experience problems. Do not risk losing irreplaceable images.

Share your images with others. Join some photo groups on Flickr; post new shots on social networking sites; assemble albums for family members; frame exceptional shots and give them as gifts. Let others enjoy the fruits of your creative life.

Let photography teach you how to live in the moment. Open all your senses to the reality of the here and now. Become more focused, less distracted. Appreciate and celebrate the natural ebb and flow of everyday life.

*A Note about Apps

As stated above, smartphones are the camera of choice for many recreational photographers. There are a wide variety of apps available for download (both free and paid) that will turn a mobile device into a portable photography studio. Users can edit or enhance images, adapt photos to create new products, add text or audio, and share their photographs almost instantly on social networking sites.

Story Starter: The Key. "Key, Dorado, Puerto Rico." (Photo by the author, Creative Commons license, some rights reserved. Retrieved from http://flickr.com/photos/dmcordell/5494763629.)

Story Starter: Teddy Bear. "The Eternal Laws of Proportion." (Photo by the author, Creative Commons license, some rights reserved. Retrieved from http://flickr.com/photos/dmcordell/7338711598.)

Smartphones and tablets can serve as mobile photo labs, portfolios, and visual notebooks. A search of Apple's App Store or Google Android Market yields a wide selection of apps that will add to the versatility of these devices. Common Sense Media has a "Best Apps and Games" page that rates and reviews apps for their educational value.

If you are planning to use apps with students, always download the app well ahead of time. Try out its features and adjust your lesson plans in the light of your experience.

Resource Box 7

Explore https://www.flickr.com/explore

National Geographic's Photo of the Day http://photography.nationalgeographic.com/photography/photo-of-the-day

National Gallery of Art—Photographs http://www.nga.gov/collection/gallery/photo.shtm

Apple App Store https://itunes.apple.com/us/genre/ios/id36?mt=8

Google Android Market https://play.google.com/store

Common Sense Media https://www.commonsensemedia.org/learning-ratings

---

Part III

Digital Images in
the Classroom

Technology and Child Development

"Technology today surrounds us and has a profound effect on how children learn as well as how educators teach."

—Susan Feld

R ecognizing the importance of media, including digital images, in the lives of our children, a number of professional associations have issued reports addressing this topic.

In January 2012, the National Association for the Education of Young Children (NAEYC) and the Fred Rogers Center for Early Learning and Children's Media at Saint Vincent College, issued a joint position statement, "Technology and Interactive Media as Tools in Early Childhood Programs Serving Children from Birth Through Age 8." Recognizing modern society's increasing reliance on "tools for communication, collaboration, social networking, and user-generated content" (p. 2), the report stressed the difference between "passive, non-interactive technology" (e.g., excessive screen time spent watching DVDs and television programs) and interactive "technology-handling skills" that foster digital literacy (p. 3).

Regarding the use of tools, for example, digital cameras, NAEYC states,

> Preschoolers have varying levels of ability to control technology and media, but with adult mediation they can demonstrate mastery of simple digital devices and are often seen using the tools as part of their pretend play. School-age children who are more proficient in using technology

can harness these tools . . . As devices and apps become more user-friendly, younger children are becoming increasingly proficient in using technological tools to accomplish a task . . . taking a photo, making a book, or engaging in other age-appropriate learning activities. (p. 6)

With a little guidance, even toddlers can take digital photos. "Portrait of Ernie." (Photo by the author, Creative Commons license, some rights reserved. Retrieved from https://www.flickr.com/photos/dmcordell/16495558298.)

A subsequent Fred Rogers Center Quality Framework Statement, issued in April 2012, noted, "Especially for children age 5 and younger, the media product should encourage joint engagement (by parents or teachers with children, by children with their siblings or peers). For older children, interactivity and engagement with the media product, including the engagement of children as creators of content, should be a priority" (p. 2).

The American Academy of Pediatrics (AAP) issued a Policy Statement, "Children, Adolescents, and the Media," in October 2013. While concerned about the potential harmful effects of media use, the AAP acknowledged, "media literacy and prosocial uses of media may enhance knowledge, connectedness, and health" (p. 2). AAP advised parents to limit total entertainment screen time, monitor their children's media activity, establish "reasonable but firm" rules for media use, and "coview TV, movies, and videos with children and teenagers . . . as a way of discussing important family values" (p. 3). Community-based pediatricians are urged to "Encourage the continuation and expansion of media education programs, or initiate implementation of media education programs in settings where they are currently lacking" (p. 4).

The Joan Ganz Cooney Center conducted a national parent survey regarding children's use of media. In January 2014, the center issued its report, "Learning at Home: Families' Educational Media Use in America," which sought to provide "understanding of the new norms of behavior among younger children and their families to help prepare educators, parents, and policymakers to promote learning and healthy development" (p. 2). Parents participating in the survey estimated that their children, ages 2 to10 years old, spend just under an hour a day consuming educational screen media [that which the parents believe is beneficial or teaches a lesson], with the majority of the activity consisting of watching TVs or DVDs (p. 10). Regarding obstacles to educational media use, "The most common reason, cited by 31% of parents whose children don't use educational media very often, is that they don't want their child using too much screen media. Another 18% of these parents say the main reason their child doesn't use educational media more often is because there are better things to do for their child's development" (p. 25). When assessing media use, the survey found that parents and children spent 25% (mobile devices, computers, video games) to 50% (TV) of their media time in joint engagement (p. 27).

The Learning in Informal and Formal Environments (LIFE) Center uses the term *joint media engagement* (JME) to "extend the notion of coviewing (parents and children watching TV together without interaction) beyond television and to more broadly describe what happens when people learn together with media" (the new coviewing: designing for learning through joint media engagement, p. 9). Through parental and teacher mediation, children should receive scaffolded practice in engaging with media, including digital images. "Joint media engagement can be a useful support for developing literacy, including basic reading ability, cultural literacy, scientific literacy, media literacy, and other 21st century skills" (p. 57).

The consensus seems to be that media use by children and young adults is neither inherently good nor bad. Type of device, duration of usage, and the nature of engagement all factor into the desirability of interacting with digital tools. It is crucial that schools offer guided practice as students work to become adept at navigating an increasingly digital world. Parents need to understand how to appropriately nurture, monitor, and support their children's technology access.

A parent interacts with her young child while watching a DVD. "Co-Viewing." (Photo by the author, Creative Commons license, some rights reserved. Retrieved from: http://flickr.com/photos/dmcordell/14848147501.)

Co-viewing involves ongoing dialogue between adult and child, whether that means parent and offspring or teacher and students. When watching TV programs or movies, this interaction might include pointing out interesting parts of the show, asking why a particular occurrence causes an emotional response, or deciding if the events could happen in real life. If these discussions take place in the home, the characters' behavior, ethics, and language could provide a natural segue to conversations about a family's belief system. Co-viewing also offers an opportunity for intergenerational fun and bonding time.

Another example of joint media engagement would be parents and children browsing through family photographs together, with adults both encouraging discussion and providing an "overarching narrative" to connect the child to the images in some way. As the child ages, encouraging him/her to design and shoot photos for a collaborative album would be a natural extension of this JME activity. "Picture walks" utilizing picture books and other facilitated readings of images are appropriate both at home and in a classroom or library setting.

While there are companies marketing digital cameras designed specifically for toddlers, the littlest users may need help in deciding what story they want to tell, framing their shots (photos of shoes and sidewalks are common in this age group), and getting the device to actually capture what they envision. Setting the camera on a table or other stable surface helps make the activity easier for small hands. In fact, special "kiddy cameras" are not really necessary at all; with supervision and a bit of guidance, even preschoolers can

Children love to look at photos of themselves as babies and are quick to recognize and name family members in an album. "Family Photos." (Photo by the author, Creative Commons license, some rights reserved. Retrieved from http://flickr.com/photos/dmcordell/16645858728.)

"The Young Photographer." (Photo by the author, Creative Commons license, some rights reserved. Retrieved from http://flickr.com/photos/dmcordell/16833429635.)

use adult point-and-shoot cameras. Older children, with their better-developed fine motor skills, are capable of independently photographing people, places, and objects, then accessing apps and online editing tools to manipulate the images they've captured.

Tweens and teens often use their cameras and mobile devices to take seemingly endless selfies to share with friends via instant messaging or on social networking sites. Far from being frivolous or narcissistic, these self-portraits represent an attempt by the subjects to present themselves in a good light, to communicate an authentic sense of who they are as individuals and how they wish others to perceive them. Selfies give adolescents control over at least a part of their life and help to build self-confidence. The comments or "likes" the selfies receive are construed as a visible sign of peer approval.

Social media can become a problem for young people (or adults, for that matter) when the desire for acceptance leads to the posting of ill-advised, suggestive, or offensive photos. With so much of their socializing being done online, teens need to continually self-monitor the quality of their interactions. Important conversations about good digital citizenship and creating a positive digital footprint, conducted both at home and in school, must necessarily include information about the appropriate, ethical use of these self-portraits as well as other digital images.

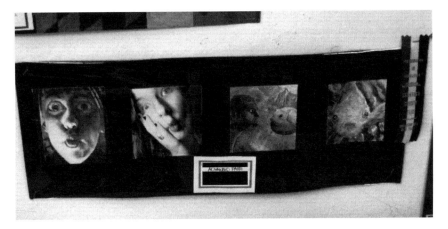

Creating a positive online presence, including archiving original products, is an important part of modern life. "Digital Footprint." (Photo by the author, Creative Commons license, some rights reserved. Retrieved from http://flickr.com/photos/dmcordell/14828225756.)

Activities and Projects

"A camera is a tool for learning how to see without a camera."
—Dorothea Lange

When constructing lesson plans for the classroom, teachers must bear in mind a number of key considerations. State and national standards have to be met, critical thinking skills stimulated, and some method of assessment included. It is important that students progress through Bloom's Taxonomy, moving from observation and the recording of images to analyzing and sorting them to the highest level of the [Revised] Taxonomy, creating meaningful new images and utilizing them in unique ways.

Common Core State Standards (CCSS) for English Language Arts (ELA), for example, require that students exhibit the "capacities of the literate individual." College and Career Readiness Anchor Standards for Speaking and Listening (CCRA.SL) specifically mention aspects of visual literacy:

- CCSS.ELA-Literacy.CCRA.SL.2
  Integrate and evaluate information presented in diverse media and formats, including visually, quantitatively, and orally.

- CCSS.ELA-Literacy.CCRA.SL.5
  Make strategic use of digital media and visual displays of data to express information and enhance understanding of presentations. (© Copyright

The Great Schools Partnership, in its Glossary of Education Reform, suggests another element: *authentic learning*:

> In education, the term authentic learning refers to a wide variety of educational and instructional techniques focused on connecting what students are taught in school to real-world issues, problems, and applications. The basic idea is that students are more likely to be interested in what they are learning, more motivated to learn new concepts and skills, and better prepared to succeed in college, careers, and adulthood if what they are learning mirrors real-life contexts, equips them with practical and useful skills, and addresses topics that are relevant and applicable to their lives outside of school.

To be "authentic," learning must:

- address real world problems with an audience beyond the classroom walls;
- utilize open-ended inquiry while searching for solutions;
- encourage social learning and community discourse; and
- take a student-directed approach to projects.

Given the opportunity to solve authentic problems, students can and will rise to the challenge. Student innovators have invented everything from a biosensor designed to quickly and easily evaluate the chemical profile of olive oil (in order to gauge its commercial quality) to a low-cost incubator model that is credited with saving the lives of premature babies born in refugee camps. At age 15, high school sophomore Jack Andraka invented an inexpensive early detection test for

Students can report sightings and contribute photos to scientific data collection sites like the Lost Ladybug Project. "A Polka-Dotted Someone." (Photo by the author, Creative Commons license, some rights reserved. Retrieved from http://flickr.com/photos/dmcordell/7310609252.)

pancreatic, ovarian, and lung cancers. Now 17, Andraka has won numerous awards, been the subject of several documentaries, spoken to audiences about STEM and education reform, and released a personal memoir. His motto is "Make something cool and change the world."

Resource Box 10

Common Core State Standards Initiative http://www.corestandards.org

Glossary of Education Reform: for Journalists, Parents, and Community Members http://edglossary.org

Authentic Learning: A Practical Introduction & Guide for Implementation http://www.ncsu.edu/meridian/win2003/authentic_learning/authentic_learning.pdf

Olive Oil Sensor Wins International Competition for Student Inventors http://news.ucdavis.edu/search/news_detail.lasso?id=11076

Student Inventor's Cheap, Portable Baby Incubator Wins Dyson Award http://www.nbcnews.com/tech/innovation/student-inventors-cheap-portable-baby-incubator-wins-dyson-award-n241251

Citizen Science: Real-World Applications for Science Students http://www.learnnc.org/lp/pages/7210

Making a Real-World Connection http://www.ascd.org/publications/books/102112/chapters/Making_a_Real-World_Connection.aspx

Jack Andraka http://jackandraka.net

Instagram is a mobile device app that allows users to take photos and share them immediately via social networking sites. "Instagram." (Photo by Jens Karlsson, Creative Commons license, some rights reserved. Retrieved from flickr.com/photos/chapter3/8101435159.)

Even younger children are able to collect data as citizen scientists or investigate issues affecting their daily lives by tracking and photographing butterflies, ladybugs, and migrating birds; addressing waste and recycling habits at home and in school; and helping to design and maintain a green space or a garden. There are museums that train junior docents to interpret exhibits for their peers. Some schools equate service projects with character education and sponsor a variety of community-oriented service and advocacy activities. In the words of Ben Franklin, "Tell me and I forget. Teach me and I remember. Involve me and I learn."

Another level of authenticity might be added by encouraging students to enter competitions that specifically target young inventors. Recognition, and sometimes cash prizes, provides an effective demonstration of how creative thinking is valued in the world outside the classroom. Student Ideas for a Better America, Discovery Education Young Scientist Challenge, Junior Science and Humanities Symposia (JSHS) Program, and Siemens Competition all sponsor such contests. Odyssey of the Mind is an international educational program that invites

Snapchat is another mobile app for sharing photos. It allows users to caption images before sending them to a social networking timeline. "Snapchat Shenanigans." (Photo by James Whatley, Creative Commons license, some rights reserved. Retrieved from flickr.com/photos/whatleydude/13456323525.)

teams of students to use creative problem-solving skills to address a variety of unusual challenges. Digital images can document the inventive process, record competition activities and publicize worthwhile projects.

There are also contests specifically for student photographers. The Sony World Photography Awards Student Focus Competition invites submissions from youths, younger than 19 years old, addressing a given theme, for example, "Enter a photo which symbolizes contemporary consumer culture." Ranger Rick's "Your Best Shots" is for children under the age of 13. Entrants may submit up to three nature photos per month to this ongoing contest for the chance to have images published in the Ranger Rick magazine. Teen Ink is "a national teen magazine, book series, and website devoted entirely to teenage writing, art, photos, and forums." Its Cover Art Contest (ages 13–19) accepts and publishes photos throughout the year. Winners have their images featured on the magazine cover and can choose from Teen Ink merchandise. The American Association of Physics Teachers (AAPT) runs a unique competition combining science and photography, the High School Physics Photo Contest. Students create visual representations of various physical concepts with accompanying explanatory text while vying for recognition and prizes.

Capturing images of themselves, their friends, and their activities is part of daily life for most young people. Popular mobile apps like Instagram and Snapchat ensure that taking and circulating photographs is as easy as writing text messages. Social networking sites make the distribution of information, in all its various formats, almost instantaneous. In today's world, students are constantly bombarded with personal and media images. Learning to accurately interpret—and ethically share—such information is a foundation skill for good digital citizenship.

Resource Box 11

Student Ideas for a Better America http://www.nmoe.org/students/siba.htm

Discovery Education Young Scientist Challenge http://www.youngscientist challenge.com

Junior Science and Humanities Symposia (JSHS) Program http://www.jshs.org

Research and Engineering Apprenticeship Program (REAP) http://www.aas -world.org/REAP/index.html

Siemens Competition https://siemenscompetition.discoveryeducation.com

Odyssey of the Mind http://www.odysseyofthemind.com

Sony World Photography Awards Student Focus Competition http://world photo.org/student-focus/2015-student-focus-competition

Ranger Rick's Your Best Shots Contest http://www.nwf.org/Kids/Ranger-Rick/Photo -Contest/Contest-Details.aspx

Teen Ink Cover Art Contest http://www.teenink.com/Contests/CoverPhotoC.php

High School Physics Photo Contest http://www.aapt.org/Programs/contests/photo contest.cfm

Social Media for Teachers: Guides, Resources, and Ideas http://www.edutopia .org/blog/social-media-resources-educators-matt-davis

---

*A Note about Social Networking in Education

Many of the ideas for these projects were inspired by or adapted from resources accessed via Twitter, Facebook, Pinterest, and other social networking sites. Educators in particular should not underestimate the value of developing a strong community of involved and innovative "colleagues" from around the world as a foundation for self-directed professional development and instructional innovation. No one person can be expert in every tool, app, and trend, but by tapping into the wisdom of the group, it is possible to benefit from the expertise of others. Social media also offer options for connecting with students, parents, and community members. It can be a strong advocacy tool at a time when schools and libraries need all the positive publicity they can garner.

Another consideration is the fact that young people spend much of their free time interacting on social media sites. Colleges and businesses use social media platforms to recruit and screen applicants. It is important that educators are able to navigate this landscape in order to model the safe and effective use of social networking for our youth.

Broadcast journalist Edward R. Murrow once said of television, "This instrument can teach, it can illuminate; yes, and it can even inspire. But it can do so only to the extent that humans are determined to use it to those ends. Otherwise it is merely wires and lights in a box." The same holds true for social media: when used thoughtfully and purposefully, it can teach, illuminate, and inspire.

When authenticity and passion are embedded in the learning process, student engagement soars. There are a number of ways photography can help foster a positive learning environment while meeting curricular goals. The following suggested visual literacy activities are grouped by theme and organized around Essential Questions. The relevant levels of Bloom's Taxonomy are also indicated for each activity.

Copyright and Fair Use

Good digital citizens act in a responsible and ethical manner when using technology. They manage their own reputations, monitor personal safety, and respect the rights of content creators as they access online resources. They understand that protecting the rights of others is a necessary part of protecting their own rights. Digital citizens are members of the world community of technology users.

"Copyright" and "fair use" are complicated concepts. While most students understand that copying an author's text without attribution is unethical, they need to extend that understanding to encompass *all* original works, including photographs, music, paintings, sculpture, even dance. These creations are automatically granted copyright protection and may not be reused or modified, except in very specific circumstances, without permission.

While it is important to respect copyright laws, students should also be aware of the other side of the coin: as creators, they might consider making their original works publicly available. By tagging, posting, and licensing their photographs and other original artifacts, they can work toward building a more fully productive, creative life. They will also be assembling a portfolio that can serve to demonstrate personal growth and showcase exceptional efforts.

Standards addressed:

- Common Core State Standards: CCSS.ELA-Literacy.CCRA.W.8

- AASL Standards for the 21st Century Learner: 3.1.6

- ISTE Standards for Students: 5

Resource Box 12

Common Core State Standards Initiative http://www.corestandards.org

AASL Standards for the 21st-Century Learner http://www.ala.org/aasl/sites/ala.org.aasl/files/content/guidelinesandstandards/learningstandards/AASL_Learning Standards.pdf

ISTE Standards for Students http://www.iste.org/docs/pdfs/20-14_ISTE_Standards-S_PDF.pdf

The New Bloom's Taxonomy http://uncw.edu/cas/documents/PickardNewBlooms Taxonomy.pdf

---

Essential Questions:

- What is digital citizenship and why is it important?
- What rights and responsibilities do students have in a digital society?
- Where can students access digital images that are copyright friendly?
- How might students legally use the original works of others?
- What is the "Creative Commons" and how does it provide a different way of protecting your work?

Activity 1: Is It Fair Use?

Bloom's levels of cognitive learning: Understand, Apply, Analyze, Evaluate

Most students are familiar with the concept of "plagiarizing," its implications, and the possible penalties for transgressions. However, they may not be as well versed in the intricacies of "fair use," which is a much less cut-and-dried concept. In the United States, the fair use doctrine sets certain specific limitations on copyright protection. Copyright law section 107 contains a list of the various purposes for which the reproduction of a particular work may be considered fair, such as "criticism, comment, news reporting, teaching, scholarship, and research."

There are four factors to be considered when determining fair use:

1. What is the purpose of the use?
2. What is the nature of the copyrighted work?
3. How much of the work will be used?
4. What is the market effect on the original work of the use?

To demonstrate how to analyze whether an adaptation is permitted, guide your students through the process. First, display a well-known copyrighted image, perhaps the Nike swish logo. Next, ask students to apply the four factors to decide whether they could legally and ethically put this logo on a school fund-raising T-shirt:

1. Purpose: to raise money
2. Nature of the work: a distinctive image
3. How much used: the complete logo but without the company name
4. Market effect: while students might not see their school shirt as a threat to the Nike corporation, point out that a company's brand is an important part of its identity and that cheap or poorly made goods bearing this brand reflect negatively on the reputation of the corporation. Wherever the swish logo is marketed commercially, Nike has received a fee and had control over the quality of the product.

Finally, decide if this instance is, in fact, a fair use of the original.

Conclusion: Putting the Nike logo on a school shirt is not fair use. A better project might involve designing and marketing original student designs.

The Walt Disney Company is known for its vigorous prosecution of anyone who makes unauthorized use of its trademark images. U.S. copyright laws have even been amended to protect Disney interests. "The [derisively labeled] Mickey Mouse Protection Act effectively 'froze' the advancement date of the public domain in the United States for works covered by the older fixed term copyright rules. Under this Act, additional works made in 1923 or afterwards that were still protected by copyright in 1998 will not enter the public domain until 2019 or afterward . . ." (Wikipedia).

After sharing this information with students, show them the video *A Fair(y) Use Tale*, a clever explanation of fair use constructed of snippets of Disney cartoons. Students may be surprised to learn that this video has been deemed fair use, since it does not affect the market value of the original films and uses the material as a parody rather than a competing work.

Conclusion: Parody of copyrighted works, even those owned by the Walt Disney Company, may sometimes be considered appropriate under "fair use."

Activity 2: Citing Sources

Bloom's levels of cognitive learning: Understand, Apply, Analyze, Evaluate

There are variations as to format but the title, creator, terms of usage, and a link should always be included when citing images. Son of Citation Machine and EasyBib are sites that can be used to generate citations for digital images in

One image, two citations:

1. (EasyBib) Bystro, Serge. European Hedgehog. Digital image. N.p., 11 July 2013. Web. <https://flic.kr/p/fbHJBb>. Some rights reserved.
2. (CogDog flickr cc generator) creative commons licensed (BY) flickr photo by Serge.By.: http://flickr.com/photos/sergebystro/9310302632

Photo citations should include a link to the creator of the image and information about terms of usage. "One Image, Two Citations." (Photo by the author, Creative Commons license, some rights reserved. Retrieved from https://www.flickr.com/photos/dmcordell/16067874243. Original image, photo by Serge Bystro, Creative Commons license, some rights reserved. Retrieved from http://flickr.com/photos/sergebystro/9310302632; text added to original image.)

the Modern Language Association (MLA), American Psychological Association (APA), Chicago, and other styles. These sites do not include usage permission, which would have to be added as an annotation. Educator Alan Levine has created a "Flickr CC attribution helper" that can be downloaded to a computer's toolbar to assist in crediting Flickr images with their proper licensing information.

Another option would be to use the website Photos for Class, a collection of school-appropriate Creative Commons–licensed images. When a specific photograph is downloaded, the site automatically generates a citation that includes both the author and the license terms. While it is permissible to download the Photos for Class images for school projects, there are some licensing restrictions, set by the creators of the works. Students under the age of 13 may only use the website under the supervision of a parent, guardian, or teacher.

Consider planning a collaborative session between classroom or subject area teachers and the school librarian to demonstrate and practice using citation-generating sites. Have students compare the Photos for Class citations with those created by another citation generator, noting similarities and differences and determining key elements necessary for an adequate, appropriate citation.

Resource Box 13

U.S. Copyright Law (Fair Use) http://www.copyright.gov/fls/fl102.html

Strategies for Fair Use (Purdue University) https://owl.english.purdue.edu/owl/resource/731/1

Copyright Term Extension Act http://en.wikipedia.org/wiki/Copyright_Term_Extension_Act

A Fair(y) Use Tale (video) http://cyberlaw.stanford.edu/blog/2007/03/fairy-use-tale

Son of Citation Machine http://old.citationmachine.net/index2.php

EasyBib http://www.easybib.com

Cog Dog's (Alan Levine's) Flickr Attribution Helper http://cogdog.github.io/flickr-cc-helper

Photos for Class http://www.photosforclass.com

Common Sense Media https://www.commonsensemedia.org/educators/curriculum

Copyright and Fair Use Animation https://www.commonsensemedia.org/videos/copyright-and-fair-use-animation

Copyright-Friendly Toolkit (from librarian Joyce Valenza) https://www.smore.com/f677-a-copyright-friendly-toolkit

Copyright Kids http://www.copyrightkids.org

Cyberbee http://www.cyberbee.com/cb_copyright.swf

Navigating the Maze: Plagiarism, Copyright, and Fair Use (wiki) http://navigatemaze.wikispaces.com

Teaching Copyright http://www.teachingcopyright.org

Understanding "Fair Use" in a Digital World (video) https://www.teachingchannel.org/videos/teaching-students-fair-use

---

An authentic outcome of this activity might be to add citation generator links and examples of properly cited resources to the school or library website.

Activity 3: Put It in Reverse

Bloom's levels of cognitive learning: Understand, Apply, Analyze, Evaluate

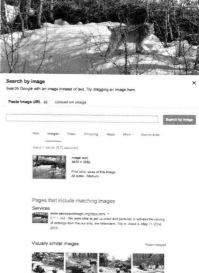

There are instances when the source of an image is unknown, making it difficult to determine whether reuse is permissible. Social networking sites frequently display interesting visuals with no identifying information. In answer to this problem, Google offers *reverse image search* capabilities that can help students track down and properly cite a photograph they are interested in utilizing.

In order to perform this type of search, users should go to the Google site, enter a keyword, and select "images" rather than web. Click on the camera icon in the search box and a "Search by images" box opens, presenting three choices: "Paste image URL," "Upload an image," or "Drag and drop an image." Once the search is initiated, Google Reverse Image attempts to locate the original photo, list any pages that include matching images, and/or suggest visually similar images.

To try out Google Reverse Image, provide the class with a few photographs to search (a little advance preparation can ensure that the test images can, in fact, be identified). Next, challenge students to find images similar to some of their own original shots. Discuss how this technique might be used to obtain copyright-friendly images to use in place of copyright-restrictive ones and to track manipulated or derivative versions of photographs.

When this photo of a lynx was dragged and dropped into Image Search, Google located both the original source and visually similar images. (Photo by the author, Creative Commons license, some rights reserved. Retrieved from http://flickr.com/photos/dmcordell/16616400609.)

Activity 4: What Is Creative Commons?

Bloom's levels of cognitive learning: Understand, Apply, Analyze, Evaluate

Copyright is the exclusive legal right of a creator to use and distribute original works, granted to ensure that the copyright holder is justly compensated for intellectual effort.

Some people choose to give their property licenses that permit reuse if certain conditions are met. Others prefer to retain full copyright protection. It is important for students to understand the different types of permissions they might encounter when searching for copyright-friendly digital images to fulfill information needs.

Creative Commons is a nonprofit organization that has released a range of licenses for free public use. Creators choose from a variety of licensing options, deciding if their property may be distributed, remixed, built upon, or used commercially. There is also a public domain dedication available by which licensees free their work for unrestricted use everywhere in the world.

Direct students to the Creative Commons (CC) site and open the "About the Licenses" page. View the short video that explains the concept of CC licenses and tools. Facilitate a discussion about the possible benefits of waiving "all rights reserved" ownership in favor of using CC designations like "Attribution," "Share Alike," "Non Commercial," and/or "No Derivative Works." Using the "Choose a License" interactive tool, explore the variety of choices possible for an original digital image. Have students decide when they might choose to retain complete copyright control (a portrait of a child or family member, a selfie) and when they would be willing to make their image available for public use (photos of historic buildings, nature shots).

Extension Activity

Creative Commons has a search page, where students can access a number of sites to locate original works that might be available for various purposes, including commercial use. Note the CC warning, *"Do not assume that the results displayed in this search portal are under a CC license."* Users must check each image selected to be sure of the exact permission terms.

Propose possible scenarios ("I need an image for my science report." "I'd like to find a photo to use in the ad I'm creating.") and have students search for photographs on two or three sites, specifying different license restrictions.

It is also possible to search for CC photos on Flickr by selecting "Only search within Creative Commons-licensed content" as an Advanced Search term. The "Explore Creative Commons" page explains more about the licenses and offers examples under each category.

Activity 5: Practice Makes Perfect

Bloom's levels of cognitive learning: Understand, Apply, Analyze

Have students choose and give a title to one of the digital images they have taken. After discussing what each alternative represents, let them select a Creative Commons license (see Activity 4 above) with the option of keeping the image fully copyright protected. Older students with Flickr accounts are able to include this information when they upload photographs to the site. Younger students and those who don't have access to Flickr can either label images collected in a folder on the school server or print out and add text to their chosen images.

Direct each student to create a citation for his/her selected digital image using the data available: name of creator, title of work, and permission license. If the photograph has been uploaded to Flickr include the hyperlink as well. The citation can be done manually or with the aid of a citation generation site (see Activity 2 above). Alternately, have students exchange information and create citations for the images of one or more of their classmates. Remind students that any subsequent use of these images should include the citation information.

Activity 6: Free for All

Bloom's levels of cognitive learning: Understand, Apply, Analyze, Evaluate

Not every student has the time, opportunity, or skill, to create original digital images for school use. If the subject of a report is historically or geographically distant, it becomes even more necessary to look elsewhere for illustrations.

Original works, including digital images, can be used without specific permission from the creator:

1. If the new usage is determined to be *fair use* (see Activity 1 above);

2. The copyright holder has waived certain rights, e.g., given the work Creative Commons licensing; or

3. The work is in the *public domain.*

Public domain photos have no known copyright restrictions. "PinkertonLincolnMcClernand." (Licensed under public domain via Wikimedia Commons. Retrieved from http://commons.wikimedia.org/wiki/File:PinkertonLincolnMcClernand.jpg#mediaviewer/File:PinkertonLincolnMcClernand.jpg.)

To help them better grasp what public domain means, have students examine the Digital Copyright Slider created by Michael Brewer and the American Library Association (ALA) Office for Information Technology Policy. After making sure that everyone understands the terminology used (and recognizes the copyright symbol), list a few possible scenarios ("image created April 30, 1989," "photo published in 1930 with no copyright notice," etc.) for students to check on the slider.

Next, visit some websites that feature public domain images. A good place to start would be Wikimedia Commons, where all images carry information about permission details, including if and why the site's administrators consider the works to be in the public domain. Wikimedia Commons is easy to search and a good source for a wide variety of useful images. Be sure to stress, however, that even public domain works may need to be credited, as explained on Wikimedia's "Commons: Reusing content outside Wikimedia" page.

Depending on students' information needs, take some time to explore public domain collections from the Smithsonian, the Public Domain Project, the Commons on Flickr (in partnership with NASA, the Library

---

Resource Box 14

Google Reverse Image Search https://support.google.com/websearch/answer/1325808?p=searchbyimagepage&hl=en

Creative Commons (CC) http://creativecommons.org/

CC Search Page http://search.creativecommons.org

About the CC Licenses http://creativecommons.org/licenses

Choose a License http://creativecommons.org/choose

Flickr Explore CC https://www.flickr.com/creativecommons

Digital Copyright Slider Created by Michael Brewer and the ALA Office for Information Technology Policy http://librarycopyright.net/resources/digitalslider

Wikimedia Commons http://commons.wikimedia.org/wiki/Main_Page

Reusing Content Outside Wikimedia http://commons.wikimedia.org/wiki/Commons:Reusing_content_outside_Wikimedia

Collect photos of community landmarks, tag, and share them publicly. "Fort Ann Central." (Photo by the author, Creative Commons license, some rights reserved. Retrieved from https://www.flickr.com/photos/dmcordell/16060712194.)

of Congress, and other participating institutions), the Library of Congress website, and World Images. Challenge each student to find an interesting public domain image from a specific event, location, or time period to share with the class.

Extension Activity

Bloom's levels of cognitive learning: Create

Create a themed public domain collection. Have students take photos of their commuity, the local environment, or the school campus. Since these images will be given a Creative Commons license, stress that no identifiable people should appear in the photos. Tag the images, locate them on a map, and make the collection available online at Flickr or some other photo archiving site via an account maintained by a teacher or an adult adviser. The owner of the account can disable comments to ensure that nothing inappropriate is posted under the images. Publicize the collection in the school and the community and on social networking sites to attract potential users.

Resource Box 15

The Smithsonian Gallery on Flickr https://www.flickr.com/photos/smithsonian

The Public Domain Project http://www.pond5.com/free

The Commons on Flickr https://www.flickr.com/commons

Library of Congress http://www.loc.gov/pictures

World Images http://worldart.sjsu.edu

---

*A Note about Permissions

Some photographers will give permission for their copyrighted work to be used in an education setting. Contact rights holders directly via e-mail to ask if they might consider allowing such an exception. Explain why and how you intend to use the image and describe any changes you might make. If you do get permission, be sure to correctly cite and link back to the creator. It's also nice to send a follow-up thank you note and a photo of the usage, if available.

Activity 7: It's O.K. to Play

Bloom's levels of cognitive learning: Apply, Create, Analyze, Evaluate

If the creator of an image grants users permission to "modify, adapt, or build upon" his/her original photograph, then it's acceptable, even encouraged, to do a bit of creative tinkering.

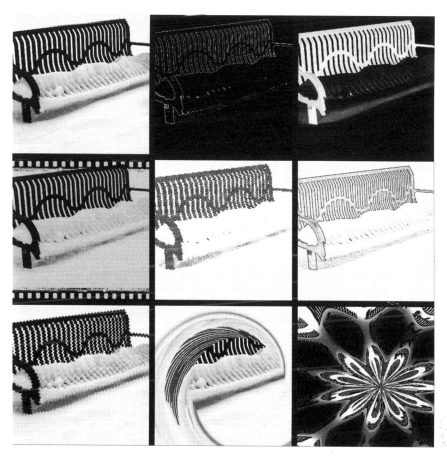

Free online photo editing sites offer an amazing variety of effects from which to choose. "One Bench Nine Ways." (Photo by the author, Creative Commons license, some rights reserved. Retrieved from https://www.flickr.com/photos/dmcordell/16495473608.)

Invite students to use their imaginations when building upon the works of others. Photo editing sites offer a variety of tools that allow users to creatively alter images. Introduce students to free online editing sites (see Activity 4, Creating & Editing Images) and then challenge them to add meaning to or alter the meaning of an image that permits modifications. Meet to compare results and analyze techniques: Does cropping, color change, a special effect, enhance or detract from the original? Will adding text reinforce the creator's "message" or change it entirely?

Extension Activity

There is a vast difference between creatively editing a photo and altering it in an attempt to deceive. While the images displayed on Snopes (see Activity 6, Reading and Responding to Images) are often blatantly false, there are numerous examples of media promotions that use altered photos to help sell a product. The Dove Self-Esteem Fund video provides an eye-opening peek at how a reasonably attractive woman is turned into a flawless paragon through the use of make-up and Photoshop editing. Use this short clip to start a conversation about ads, self-image, and the ethics of image manipulation.

Reading and Responding to Images

Standards addressed:

- Common Core State Standards: CCSS.ELA-Literacy.CCRA.R.7
- AASL Standards for the 21st Century Learner: 1.1.6
- ISTE Standards for Students: 3b

Essential Questions:

- What stories may pictures tell?
- How do you communicate with images?
- How can an artist/illustrator/photographer influence the way people think?
- Do photographs ever lie? How?

Activity 1: Picture Walk

Bloom's levels of cognitive learning: Understand, Apply, Analyze, Evaluate, Create

Picture books offer the perfect introduction to reading images for even the youngest learners. They provide, for many children, their first experience with art and formalized storytelling. Illustrations, whether drawn or photographed, can be used to elicit reflections about theme, characters, and setting. They encourage listeners to tap into critical thinking skills to create their own narratives, based on what they are seeing.

A *picture walk* is designed to "preview" a story. After naming the title and author of a book, the teacher or librarian displays the cover and asks for predictions about what will happen. Flipping through the book without reading the text, the teacher encourages students to explore meaning through dialogue with their peers. Simple, open-ended questions like "Who is this?" "How does this make you feel?" "What do you think might happen next?" help participants to focus on visual cues. Once the picture walk has been completed, the teacher should read the text and solicit reactions, comparing and contrasting the students' interpretations of the images to what the author actually wrote. The Caldecott Medal (given for excellence in illustrating children's books) winners and honors lists are good places to find books suitable for picture walks.

A picture walk helps students more fully engage with both stories and illustrations. "Picture Walk." (Photo by the author, Creative Commons license, some rights reserved. Retrieved from http://flickr.com/photos/dmcordell/15269800042.)

Among the Caldecott selections are a number of wordless books. As with other picture walks, encourage students to voice their interpretations as each page is examined. Direct their attention to visual clues, like expressions on the characters' faces, the mood created by colors and style, and the details of the setting. Return to the story a second time and invite students to add spoken narrative and dialogue to what they are seeing. Let individuals pick out what they feel is a key image and explain how it helped their understanding of the story. Invite volunteers to "read" the book to classmates.

Variations

- With older students, it might be fun to "flip" the picture walk. The teacher could read the text of a story without showing the illustrations and have learners provide their own original images. Alternately, students could take photographs to "re-illustrate" a story.

- After a picture walk using a wordless book, let students re-create the story as a writing activity.

- Turn the picture walk into a critical thinking "game." Create a simple spinner or cube to roll (see how to create a paper photo cube, Activity 11, Creating and Editing images, but substitute text for images) with some Why? What if? and How? questions, for example, "Why did that happen?" "What would happen if the setting were different?" "How would I behave in that situation?" Have students answer whichever question comes up when it's their turn to play.

- Amp the critical thinking game up a notch: put words like "why, what, what if, how, describe, compare" on the spinner or cube. When it's their turn, students use the word that comes up to frame a question that classmates must answer.

- Another way for students to respond to a wordless book is to have them take photos of the pages, assemble them in a slideshow, and then add narration with an app like Shadow Puppet (free), Story Creator (free), or SonicPics (paid).

Please note that if you are photographing the pages of a copyrighted work for this or any other activity, there may be legal restrictions regarding using the images (and/or text) without the author's and illustrator's permissions. Sharing any student projects that contain copyrighted material, within their district, or even as part of a conference presentation, is probably allowable; posting a video to YouTube is definitely not.

Resource Box 17

The Dos and Don'ts of a Picture Walk http://readingiselementary.blogspot.com/2013/02/the-dos-and-donts-of-picture-walk.html

The Picture Walk http://readingtokids.org/ReadingClubs/TipPictureWalk.php

Caldecott Medal http://www.ala.org/alsc/awardsgrants/bookmedia/caldecottmedal/caldecotthonors/caldecottmedal

2nd Graders Narrate Wordless Books with the Shadow Puppet App http://linkis.com/blogspot.com/vo2qu

Shadow Puppet https://itunes.apple.com/us/app/shadow-puppet/id700902833?mt=8

Story Creator https://itunes.apple.com/ie/app/story-creator/id545369477?mt=8

SonicPics https://itunes.apple.com/us/app/sonicpics/id345295488?mt=8

What Does Copyright Law and Fair Use Have to Say About a School or Library Recording Audio Narration of a Book, and/or Reading and Showing Pictures from a Book on YouTube? http://www.quora.com/What-does-copyright-law-and-fair-use-have-to-say-about-a-school-or-library-recording-audio-narration-of-a-book-and-or-reading-and-showing-pictures-from-a-book-on-YouTube

---

Activity 2: How to Read a Graphic Novel

Bloom's levels of cognitive learning: Understand, Apply, Analyze, Evaluate

Graphic novels use sequential images to tell a well-developed story. Readers of all abilities, including those who are reluctant or ESL (English as Second Language) learners, are attracted to this very popular format.

Graphic novels require a different approach to reading, according to Boston University researcher Laura Jiménez:

- First, skim the book, noting style and design elements.

- Next, examine the first page more closely to determine setting, main characters, and genre. Both of these steps can be done as an individual or group activity in the classroom.

- Once students have read the entire book, provide them with time to reflect on their experience. Ask, "Did the text and illustrations work cohesively to tell a story?" "Would this have worked better as text only?" "Why do you think the author decided to write this as a graphic novel?"

Practice using this method as a group activity, then let students select and read a graphic novel on their own. Challenge them to come up with a personal analysis of why and how graphic novels have value in a classroom and library.

With older students, introduce them to the Pulitzer Prize–winning graphic novel *Maus*, by Art Spiegelman. This semi-biographical graphic work is set during the Holocaust and depicts the Jewish population as mice and Germans as cats. Discuss why Spiegelman chose to represent different groups as animals and whether this strategy enhances or detracts from the story he tells.

Extension Activity

Many classic novels are now available in a graphic novel format. Have students read both versions of *A Tale of Two Cities*, for example, and then compare and contrast the reading experiences. Extend the exercise further by viewing scenes from a movie version of the same novel.

Activity 3: Close Reading of Photographs

Bloom's levels of cognitive learning: Understand, Apply, Analyze, Evaluate

Students are expected to be skilled in accessing, analyzing, verifying, and utilizing information. Close reading, a purposeful sifting of data for meaning, applies to images as well as text.

One way to practice this skill with students is by having them examine photographs published in magazines and newspapers. Select a current events topic and display a relevant photo, concealing its caption. In groups or individually, ask students to assess the message it conveys by considering the following questions:

- Who is the intended audience?

- What visual "clues" led you to this conclusion?

- Does the photo use logic, emotion, or both to deliver its message?

- Did the photographer employ any techniques (angle, lighting, focal point) to add impact to the image?

- Does this image convey a definite point of view?

- Do you think that this photograph has been edited? Why or why not?

After sharing student analyses, reveal the caption and take note of the similarities or dissimilarities between the actual text and the group's interpretations of the photo. Extend the activity by selecting multiple shots of the same event, from different sources, to compare and contrast.

Extension Activity

The *New York Times* Learning Network is an online current events news site for grades 3–12. On Mondays during the school year, the site publishes a *Times* photo without a caption, headline, or other information about its origins, for classroom discussion. Students are asked to consider three questions: "What's going on in this picture?" "What do you see that makes you say that?" "What more can you find?" On Tuesday, the *Times* reveals more information about the image and places it in context. Help students polish their close reading skills by including the "What's Going On in This Picture?" activity in weekly lesson plans.

Activity 4: Name This Photo

Bloom's levels of cognitive learning: Understand, Apply, Analyze, Evaluate

On a bulletin board or classroom wall, hang a few printouts of photographs with a strong storytelling element, for example, images from the Library of Congress website or Flickr collection.

Have students study the gallery, then write their suggestions for titles on sticky notes to be placed under the appropriate image. If desired, the teacher can also have students indicate their favorite titles by either a show of hands or the use of sticky dots. Discuss why each title is or is not appropriate for the visual content of the photo to which it is attached. Reveal the original descriptions of the photographs and compare what was actually going on to what viewers perceive is happening.

Optional Pre-Activity

Prior to the naming activity, select one photo for whole-group analysis. Have students brainstorm lists of nouns, verbs, adjectives, and adverbs that describe the image. After reflecting on the word choices, have each student write a sentence describing the photograph. Use these descriptive sentences to generate a list of possible titles.

Variation

Post the photo gallery on a Padlet and let students record their name choices there.

Activity 5: Color My World

Bloom's levels of cognitive learning: Understand, Analyze, Evaluate, Create

Colorization is a process that adds color to black-and-white or sepia photographs or films. Colorizing vintage images can make them appear more realistic to modern viewers. Show students some "before and after" colorized photos of famous people, like Abraham Lincoln and Albert Einstein. Have them analyze their reactions to the altered shots and decide whether the changes enhance or detract from the original.

Next, invite students to edit a photo, one of their own or a CC image, changing it from color to black and white. Compare the two versions; decide which is more effective and why. Ask the group to consider how subject matter and personal preference enter into the decision as to whether black and white or color is better for a specific shot.

True colorization of photographs is a very labor-intensive process involving working with color adjustment in different areas of an image. Older students, familiar with using Adobe Photoshop, might be interested in attempting to colorize vintage photos.

Activity 6: Is It Real or Is It a Hoax?

Bloom's levels of cognitive learning: Understand, Apply, Analyze, Evaluate

A natural follow-up to the close reading activity would be showing students where they might search to determine the validity of a photograph when internal clues are inconclusive.

The best-known website for this purpose is Snopes. The site's Fauxtography page reminds visitors "Numerous photographs and videos circulate on the Internet. Some are real. Some are fake. Some are real but have been given false backstories."

Users type in a search term and select a link from the results. For example, "shark" returns 40 hits with brief summaries. Clicking on "Does a photograph

---

Resource Box 18

Using Graphic Novels with Children and Teens (tips and recommendations from Scholastic) http://www.scholastic.com/graphix_teacher/pdf/Graphix%20Teachers%20guide.pdf

Graphic Novel Adaptations of Classic Books http://www.goodreads.com/list/show/34639.Graphic_Novel_Adaptations_of_Classic_Books

Analyzing Photographs (J. Paul Getty Museum) http://www.getty.edu/education/teachers/classroom_resources/curricula/exploring_photographs/background1.html

What's Going On in This Picture? (*New York Times*) http://learning.blogs.nytimes.com/category/lesson-plans/whats-going-on-in-this-picture

Library of Congress on Flickr https://www.flickr.com/photos/library_of_congress

Padlet https://padlet.com

40 Incredible Colorized Photos from History http://www.vintag.es/2015/03/40-incredible-colorized-photos-from.html

How to Colorize Black and White Vintage Photographs in Photoshop http://www.howtogeek.com/howto/42066/how-to-colorize-black-and-white-vintage-photographs-in-photoshop

Snopes Fauxtography http://www.snopes.com/photos/photos.asp

---

show a shark attacking a British Navy diver?" brings up a photo with a detailed analysis of whether the image is a true one. Either print out a number of Snopes photos or show cropped versions of the pages to students and challenge them to identify which of the three categories is correct for the image. Refer to Snopes to prove or disprove their conclusions.

Activity 7: Five-Photo Stories

Bloom's levels of cognitive learning: Analyze, Apply, Create

A five-photo story is a sequence of images that relate a complete story without the use of text, a sort of abbreviated wordless book. A teacher might structure the activity by specifying that the images students select must include the setting (time or place), a main character, a supporting character or antagonist, a problem, and a solution.

There are a number of other ways that the five-photo story can be adapted for classroom use:

This sequence of images relates the story of the birth of a turtle. "5-Photo Turtle Story." (Photo by the author, Creative Commons license, some rights reserved. Retrieved from http://flickr.com/photos/dmcordell/15285189376.)

- Students draw five photographs from a "deck" printed out by the teacher. They are given a certain amount of time in which to use these images to create a coherent story, which they later share with the class. The teacher can structure the activity by specifying that the images must include the setting, a main character, a supporting character or antagonist, a problem, and a solution. An online variation is to create a folder containing numbered photos and assign random numbers to each student ("Tim, you use #1, 3, 4, 8, and 11") to use in constructing a story.

- The teacher posts five photographs on a bulletin board and has students use the same images, but in whatever order they wish, to tell a story.

- Students use digital devices to take their own photos and then select five of them to create a narrative.

- The teacher provides four photographs and challenges students to complete the "story" verbally or with a fifth photo, either their own shot or one from Creative Commons.

Extension Activity

Have students add spoken narrative to their own or a classmate's five-photo story. See Activity 1 above for examples of how to do this.

Activity 8: Visual Writing Prompts

Bloom's levels of cognitive learning: Analyze, Apply, Create

Rather than text prompts, students are given a visual prompt and then asked to "Tell the story" it represents to them.

The Literacy Shed offers free "images to inspire writing," along with some key questions to consider. Pinterest boards are another good source of photo prompts. Author M. J. Bronstein's book *Photoplay!* features photographs with empty white space where readers are invited to draw what is missing: "Design an upside-down world, a passing parade, and an underwater garden. Draw a tasty birthday cake for Bob, a pet for Grace, and Ravi's imaginary friend . . ." Some of Bronstein's images are available for free download from Chronicle Books and could easily serve as visual writing prompts.

"Window: What Does She See?" (Photo by the author, Creative Commons license, some rights reserved. Retrieved from http://flickr.com/photos/dmcordell/14486995381.)

Extension Activity

Bloom's levels of cognitive learning: Create

Have students take turns providing visual writing prompts for their classmates. These could be images found through an online search, cut from magazines or newspapers, or taken by the students themselves. (Be sure to preview choices before allowing them to be presented to the class.)

Sometimes a simple image can be used as a great story starter. "That Which Was Lost."
(Photo by the author, Creative Commons license, some rights reserved. Retrieved from
https://www.flickr.com/photos/dmcordell/16681857111.)

Resource Box 19

Story in 5 Photos http://maps.playingwithmedia.com/story-in-5-photos

Creative Commons http://search.creativecommons.org

Visual Writing Prompts http://visualwritingprompts.wordpress.com

Literacy Shed http://www.literacyshed.com/the-images-shed.html

Photo Prompts (Pinterest board) http://www.pinterest.com/PinsFromMcTeach/photo
-prompts

Photo Play! By M. J. Bronstein (free download) http://www.chroniclebooks.com/
landing-pages/pdfs/photoplay-chronicle-books.pdf

Creating and Editing Images

Standards addressed:

- Common Core State Standards: CCSS.ELA-Literacy.CCRA.SL.2
- AASL Standards for the 21st Century Learner: 4.1.3, 4.1.8
- ISTE Standards for Students: 1a, 1b

Essential Questions:

- How is photography used to communicate in our society?
- What are the qualities of an effective photograph?

- How can varied effects be applied successfully to a composition to produce effective communication of ideas?

- How will the images people create reflect who they are?

- How do people engage in the visual arts throughout their lives?

*A Note about Parent Permissions and Other Practical Considerations

Photographers need to always be mindful of the rights of individuals with respect to having an identifiable picture of them taken and shared. This especially holds true in a school setting. Some districts require signed parental permission before any photos of their minor children are published (Opt In); others assume consent unless a parent specifically denies permission (Opt Out). It is important to understand and comply with your district's policies.

Since few children under the age of 13 have individual Flickr or similar online photo storage site accounts (there is a Yahoo/Flickr family option, which requires parents to register their child), teachers need to plan how student-generated images will be collected and uploaded. Where only school equipment is being used, it is relatively simple to upload photos to a shared school file or to an account registered to an individual teacher. If students are using their own devices, they can save images to the camera's memory card and upload at school or they can upload images on home computers and mail them to a designated school address.

When instructing younger learners, some teachers choose to avoid complications by either providing preselected images for editing and other projects or allowing students to search online for copyright-friendly photos that they can utilize. Older students can create their own folders of saved photos on the district server.

Another alternative is to allow students to search for images via Creative Commons, a well-known source of usable content with clearly indicated copyright licenses. Please note that some CC images may not be suitable for student use.

Activity 1: Classroom Photographer

Bloom's levels of cognitive learning: Apply, Evaluate, Create

Many elementary teachers assign jobs to their students as a means of fostering responsibility. A "class photographer" could perform a number of tasks:

- create a visual schedule or calendar;

- capture special events (Flag Day celebration, birthday parties, assemblies);

- document products and projects completed by fellow classmates;

- contribute to a file of photos for an end-of-the-year memory book or slideshow;

- add to a databank of informal photos that will be archived for use in their high school yearbook; and

- go on special assignments: create visual prompts for a special education teacher, take photos for the district newsletter, photograph menu items for the cafeteria staff.

Encourage students to photograph a variety of school activities, like this dress-up corner at a library book fair. "Starz." (Photo by the author, Creative Commons license, some rights reserved. Retrieved from https://www.flickr.com/photos/dmcordell/16479876217.)

At the beginning of the school year, give a general overview of what the job entails. Before sending him/her out on assignment, be sure that the chosen photographer understands how to use the camera provided. Older students should also be able to upload, tag, and store photos in a folder designated by the teacher.

Activity 2: Photowalk

Bloom's levels of cognitive learning: Apply, Evaluate, Create

During a photowalk, a group of participants walk together on a predetermined route, using their cameras to record whatever captures their interest. Most photowalks have a theme, although it is considered acceptable to include other shots as well. A class photowalk could take place anywhere—inside the classroom, in the community, or on a fieldtrip—and is a suitable activity for all age levels.

Possible photowalk themes might include the following:

- Letter/number/shapes/colors walk: Students practice their observation skills by locating and photographing individual letters, numbers, or geometric shapes.

This garden sundial displays a number of angles and curves. "Sundial." (Photo by the author, Creative Commons license, some rights reserved. Retrieved from https://www.flickr.com/photos/dmcordell/16475941787.)

Images taken on nature walks can be identified when students return to the classroom. "British Soldiers." (Photo by the author, Creative Commons license, some rights reserved. Retrieved from https://www.flickr.com/photos/dmcordell/16063148673.)

- Nature walk: One option is to have students take pictures of wildflowers, plants, or insects, then identify them after they have returned to the classroom. A fun follow-up project is to create nature guides for other students to use, perhaps as a collaborative project, with different classrooms or grade levels

Observant photo walkers will discover unexpected points of interest in every community. "Wings of Stone." (Photo by the author, Creative Commons license, some rights reserved. Retrieved from https://www.flickr.com/photos/dmcordell/16495495148.)

Photographs taken in cemeteries help to document local history and aid genealogists in their search for family information. This monument was erected by bereaved parents, who mourned the loss of their two young sons in the American Civil War. "Left on the Field." (Photo by the author, Creative Commons license, some rights reserved. Retrieved from https://www.flickr.com/photos/dmcordell/16496905349.)

focusing on diverse flora and fauna, then coming together to compile a local nature encyclopedia. The project could be expanded even further by sharing these images with other schools around the country or around the world.

- Community walk: Take a hometown tour, snapping local businesses, landmarks, architecture, homes. Use the photos in a slideshow or brochure to document local history.

- Cemetery walk: Respectfully tour a local burial ground. Try to capture the different styles of headstones, interesting inscriptions, historic markers (usually on the graves of veterans), and unusual names. Not only will such a field trip offer an interesting perspective on history—and genealogy—but it might also provide a community service by helping to digitally preserve deteriorating gravestones. If there is no local database of headstone images, students might create one as a public service project or consider adding their photos to the popular Find a Grave website.

- School walk: Sometimes people don't really "see" until they view the world through a camera. Direct students to capture interesting and unusual perspectives of their school environment. Turn the exercise into a game, and challenge students, staff, and even visiting parents to correctly label a photo gallery of odd angles, hidden nooks, and dusty objects located throughout the district. Or have teachers go on a school photowalk, then send their students out on a hunt to track down the location of each item or area photographed.

Variation

Send students on a nature scavenger hunt, trying to find and photograph items on a list provided by the teacher (lichen, a maple leaf, milkweed pods, etc.). Even better, make the list a visual one, a series of photos that show what objects are being sought. As students find each item, they take a photo, including either themselves (in a selfie) or a token (their hat, a name tag, etc.) in the digital image. Any field trip, including a visit to an indoor venue like a museum, could include this type of visual scavenger hunt.

Activity 3: 50 Things

Bloom's levels of cognitive learning: Understand, Apply, Analyze, Evaluate, Create

In order to compile a list of similar items, it is necessary to identify their unique qualities. For this project, the teacher selects a theme and indicates the number of images that

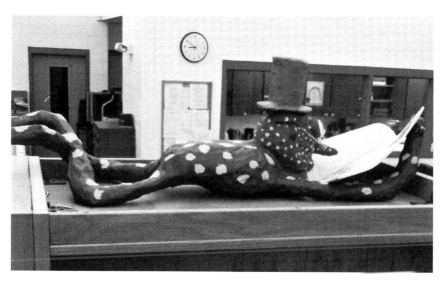

Sometimes objects hide in plain sight. Visitors must look up to see this library mascot. "Reading Creature." (Photo by the author, Creative Commons license, some rights reserved. Retrieved from https://www.flickr.com/photos/dmcordell/16495546408.)

students, singly or in groups, must provide to illustrate that theme. In order to foster higher-level thinking skills, students should be required to analyze and express, either verbally or in a reflective writing piece, the commonalities that link their chosen artifacts.

The images for this activity could be found via a keyword search in Creative Commons or created by students as part of a digital photography assignment. One local newspaper ran a series of "50 Objects that Define Our County."

Other themes to consider include the following:

Use visual cues for a museum scavenger hunt. "Can You Find Me?" (Photo by the author, Creative Commons license, some rights reserved. Retrieved from http://flickr.com/photos/dmcordell/ 15258984841.)

- 10 objects that represent me

- 20 landmarks that define my town

- 10 artifacts that I would include in a time capsule

- 7 special things that tell the story of my family

- 12 objects that represent what Thanksgiving means to me

- 9 items that I would include in an emergency readiness kit (this could easily expand into a discussions of disaster preparedness and culminate in the creation of home emergency kits)

- 5 things no home should be without

- 15 places I want to visit in my life (a visual bucket list)

Variation

Have students photograph and share the images of a set number of objects without revealing the theme. Challenge classmates to correctly identify what these objects have in common—another exercise that provides practice in analysis and evaluation.

Activity 4: I Spy

Bloom's levels of cognitive learning: Apply, Create

"I spy with my little eye . . ." is one of the first games that children learn to play. It requires no equipment, just a minimum of two players, one of whom gives clues while the other tries to guess or "spy" the object being described.

The basic premise can easily be adapted for use in the classroom by creating a bulletin board display, collage, or self-published book based on the familiar game. To begin, have students gather an assortment of small objects, then arrange them on a flat surface and take photos. The shots could be themed or display a random assortment. Supply clues or a list to help viewers locate specific items.

Sharpen observation powers with this popular guessing game. "I Spy with My Little Eye." (Photo by Robert Couse-Baker, Creative Commons license, some rights reserved. Retrieved from http://flickr.com/photos/29233640@N07/7854678628.)

Variation

Play the game in a foreign language class, with the list of objects in the language being studied. Or with ESL students, have them identify the item in both their native tongue and in English.

Activity 5: Fun with Language

Bloom's levels of cognitive learning: Analyze, Apply, Create

Photographer Kate TerHaar mixes tiny figurines with normal-sized everyday objects, takes a macro photo, and then adds a witty title, often in the form of a pun. After sharing TerHaar's *Small* Flickr album with students, challenge them to create similar vignettes. The dollhouse department of a craft store or the model railroad section of a hobby shop is the perfect place to buy some miniature props to share with the class.

Variations

Visually portray figures of speech (simile, hyperbole, understatement, etc.) or abstract concepts like contentment, peace, joy, or determination. If students are unsure how to approach this assignment, do a pre-search of Creative Commons to find examples.

Use photos to convey abstract concepts in unusual ways. "Strength." (Photo by the author, Creative Commons license, some rights reserved. Retrieved from http://flickr.com/photos/dmcordell/16615159650.)

Resource Box 20

Creative Commons in K–12 Education http://www.edutopia.org/creative-commons-k-12-education

Photowalks: The Art of Observation (blog posting) http://dmcordell.blogspot.com/2012/07/photowalks-art-of-observation.html

Lost Ladybug Project http://www.lostladybug.org

Journey North (global study of wildlife migration and seasonal change by Annenberg Learner) http://www.learner.org/jnorth

Cemeteries wiki (includes a "curricular connections" page) http://cemeteries.wikispaces.com/home

Find a Grave http://www.findagrave.com

Small, a Flickr Album https://www.flickr.com/photos/katerha/sets/72157625976037087

Activity 6: Photo Editing

Bloom's levels of cognitive learning: Apply, Analyze, Evaluate, Create

While some photographers take pride in sharing "raw" (unprocessed) images, photo editing provides the opportunity for creativity and fun. Students bring their critical thinking skills into play as they apply elements of design to the images they capture. Exploring the possibilities of photo editing can lead to thoughtful conversations about photo hoaxes and the retouched photos that are seen daily via modern media.

It's best to start with simple edits. Begin by letting students work on an image or set of images preselected by the teacher. Have them try cropping the photo. Study the results and compare the clarity and sharpness of images cropped to varying degrees. Ask students if they can think of better ways to take close-ups (move nearer to the object being photographed, use the macro option, attach a special lens, etc.). Point out that the best use of cropping is to highlight certain details or eliminate distracting, nonessential ones.

Editing helps to correct overexposure and emphasize interesting details in this photo of a graffiti-covered park bench. "Graffiti Bench." (Photo by the author, Creative Commons license, some rights reserved. Retrieved from http://flickr.com/photos/dmcordell/15250365988.)

before

after

Holiday special effects edits turn a staid historic home into a creepy haunted house. "The James L. Dix House." (Photo by the author, Creative Commons license, some rights reserved. Retrieved from http://flickr.com/photos/dmcordell/15250368428.)

Next, let students experiment with exposure and color adjustments. Convert color images to black and white, then decide which option is more effective for a particular image and why, keeping in mind that different editing techniques are appropriate for different photos. Play with adding borders, text, stickers, and special effects. Encourage students to analyze the results of their edits, then apply what they've learned to the original photographs they capture, whether in school or in their extracurricular life.

It isn't necessary to be a Photoshop expert to achieve a quality product; free online sites offer a lot of editing options:

- PicMonkey: Edit photos and create collages. Students upload images from their computer, then adjust exposure, switch from color to black and white, add text, and much more. The new "Shape Cutouts" in the Frames section could be used to create circular images for International Dot Day (staged to encourage people of all ages to harness their creativity), hearts for Valentine's Day, stars for Flag Day, etc. Edited photos may be saved to a computer and also shared via Facebook, Twitter, Pinterest, Flickr, Tumblr, or e-mail. The Themes option offers overlays, stickers, and other fun tools for seasonal fun.

- Ribbet: Online photo editing with some interesting effects. Images can be uploaded from the computer, Flickr, Facebook, Picasa, Google+, a webcam, or a website. Once an account is created, users have access to their editing history and are able to revisit and re-edit uploaded images. One engaging activity might be to upload a selfie, then use seasonal editing options to add playful features, like a fake beard, zombie makeup, or funhouse mirror distortions.

- FotoFlexer: In addition to standard photo editing effects, this site offers a layering (superimposing one image on top of another) function. Images may be uploaded from a computer or retrieved from Flickr, Facebook, and other social networking sites. It is not possible to print directly from the site, but images may be saved to a desktop and printed from there. Edited images may also be shared with selected sites or e-mailed.

- Pixlr: The online site Pixlr Editor has both photo editing and image creation options. Two apps, Pixlr Express (free) and Pixlr-o-matic ($0.99), allow users to do simple edits and add effects to photos taken with their mobile devices.

- Pablo: Quickly create images to share on social networking sites. Type in text or choose from preloaded quotations, then add stock images or upload your own photographs as a background. After selecting from a few editing options, users can share their creation on Twitter or Facebook or download to post on other websites. While the products created on Pablo are limited in scope, it provides an easy way to create a mini-poster.

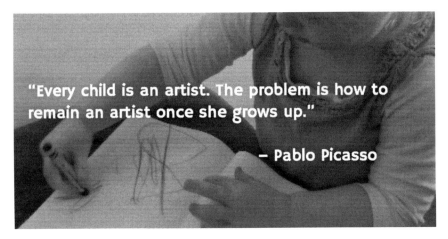

It is easy to combine text and images on this site. "Created with Pablo." (Photo by the author, Creative Commons license, some rights reserved. Retrieved from http://flickr.com/photos/dmcordell/16213485003.)

Activity 7: It's a Blur

Bloom's levels of cognitive learning: Apply, Analyze, Evaluate, Create

For a variety of reasons, it might not be possible to obtain permission before using a photo that includes a recognizable face. There are a number of solutions to this problem. Have students experiment with a photograph from a class event or field trip to decide which options they feel are the most effective in disguising faces. In addition, have them practice setting up photos to minimize the need for image manipulation.

Possible ways to shield identities include the following:

1. Crop the person out of the photo;

2. Photograph people from behind, at an angle, or in silhouette, to mask their identities; or

3. Edit with a pixelate tool on a photo-editing site like Ribbet or PicMonkey.

If cell phones are allowed in the classroom, consider demonstrating apps specifically designed to blur features. The iTunes store offers a number of options, both free and paid, that enable users to blur selected areas of an image. This might be a good option to discuss with older students, since they are more likely to take and post photos on their mobile devices.

Activity 8: Makerspaces

Bloom's levels of cognitive learning: Apply, Analyze, Evaluate, Create

June 18, 2014, was designated the first National Day of Making in the United States. President Barack Obama proclaimed, "Together, let us unleash the imagination of our people, affirm that we are a Nation of makers, and ensure that the next great technological revolution happens right here in America."

Makerspaces provide a place to tinker and explore new ideas. Whether the "tools" being used are high (3D printers) or low (knitting needles) tech, the important thing is that users are given an opportunity to tap into their creativity. Makers continually exercise critical thinking and problem-solving skills as they work to produce a unique product. In a society where entrepreneurship is valued, access to a makerspace means that students are able to gain hands-on experience in design and innovation.

A photography makerspace might simply consist of a digital camera available for student use, a laptop with editing sites bookmarked, and/or an iPad with photo apps. Make sure that students know how to operate the camera, download photos, access and use editing options, and save images to folders. Producing instructional brochures or videos could be an interesting and useful project for some of the makers to tackle.

Editing is a form of creating. Once edited, images can be used in an almost endless number of ways, from making a calendar or book to decorating a wide assortment of objects. Set aside some class time to share and discuss students' personal portfolios of images. Use student photos for events posters, public service announcements, and district newsletters. Have a gallery showing and invite other classes to view the photographs. In addition to hanging photographic prints, display other products that have been enhanced with original images. Celebrate photography for the art form that it is.

There are a number of ways to mask the identity of the person in a photo. This student's face was pixelated on a photo-editing site; her name on the diploma was also covered. "Pixelated." (Photo by the author, Creative Commons license, some rights reserved. Retrieved from http://flickr.com/photos/dmcordell/16683130745.)

Taking a photo from behind or from a distance effectively masks identities. "The Ball Boy." (Photo by the author, Creative Commons license, some rights reserved. Retrieved from https://www.flickr.com/photos/dmcordell/16475930137.)

Capturing silhouettes is another way to avoid the problem of needing to obtain permission to photograph an adult or child. "Atlanta Aquarium." (Photo by the author, Creative Commons license, some rights reserved. Retrieved from https://www.flickr.com/photos/dmcordell/16681744021.)

Resource Box 21

PicMonkey http://www.picmonkey.com

International Dot Day http://www.thedotclub.org/dotday

Ribbet http://www.ribbet.com

FotoFlexer http://fotoflexer.com

Pixlr http://pixlr.com

Pablo https://bufferapp.com/pablo

Images can be used to produce an endless variety of products. "Photography Projects." (Photo by the author, Creative Commons license, some rights reserved. Retrieved from http://flickr.com/photos/dmcordell/15258891481.)

Pinterest is a wonderful source of project ideas. Use keywords like "photo projects," "photos in the classroom," and "things to make with photos" to search for inspiration, then start your own board to showcase photos of completed student projects.

Some websites that offer Maker options include the following:

- Canva: This design-oriented site invites users to create "album covers, book covers, brochures, cards, flyers, infographics, photo collages, posters, presentations, and social graphics." There are tutorials and teaching materials available with lesson plans and examples of how Canva can be used in the classroom.

- BigHugeLabs: Upload photos or link to Flickr to access images and albums. Create mosaics, posters, and more. The Trading Card generator might be used in a variety of projects. For example, have students upload a photo and then add information to create decks of people, places, and things.

- phrase.it: On this free site, users upload a photo and add speech bubbles. Students could create conversations about almost any topic, from good

Make a collage, add speech bubbles, and deliver your message in an engaging way. Keep to a black and white palette if planning to print and distribute the product. "Pumpkin Phrase It." (Photo by the author, Creative Commons license, some rights reserved. Retrieved from http://flickr.com/photos/dmcordell/16682110702.)

digital citizenship to upcoming school events. By creating a collage first, then adding the bubbles, students are able to produce photo comic strips. (See also Activity 3, Digital Storytelling.)

- Zazzle and Café Press: These commercial sites allow people to create custom clothing, calendars, totes, and a variety of other products for fund-raisers, gifts, and personal use. Simply upload a photo and choose from the styles, fabrics, and colors offered. While students could make something and actually purchase it, there are other ways to use the sites. An "entrepreneur" learning unit could challenge individuals or small groups to form a business, produce a product like a T-shirt, create a business card, and market their product to the class. Both shirts and cards can be customized online, with screenshots capturing the items for printout and display.

Following are a few photo apps to consider for classroom use (be sure to preview and try out apps before using them with students or recommending them to parents):

- Elmer's Photo Patchwork: This paid app provides line drawings and patchwork templates. The user taps each section of the patchwork to take and upload a photo that can be themed (nature, garden, home) or random. The final product is an elephant-shaped collage. This activity is based on the children's picture book series *Elmer the Patchwork Elephant* by David McKee.

- Kuddle: A free app that has been described as the Instagram for children and young teens. Member of this social networking site can share and caption their own photos, but comments are not allowed (to forestall any online bullying). Contents are moderated and parents/caregivers are able to monitor their children's activity. With parental approval, Kuddle might be a good way to introduce students to responsible digital citizenship.

- Priime: Free photo editing app with filters in the style of famous photographers. Easily access photos already in your device's photo library; once edited, you can store the images or return to undo changes. Suitable for most ages up to adult.

- FrameMagic: Paid photo editing app that allows users to turn their photographs and videos into a photo collage, video collage, or video slideshow. Described by reviewers as "user friendly," FrameMagic is a simple mobile creativity app.

- Little Story Creator: This app is a free digital scrapbooking and photo collage maker. Students could use its tools to edit photos, add audio, and create and share visual stories.

Resource Box 22

The Importance of Makerspaces http://learni.st/users/dawncasey/boards/33414
-the-importance-of-makerspaces

The Philosophy of Educational Makerspaces http://www.teacherlibrarian.com/
2014/06/18/educational-makerspaces

Pinterest http://www.pinterest.com

Canva Teaching Materials https://designschool.canva.com/teaching-materials

BigHuge Labs http://bighugelabs.com

phrase.it http://phrase.it

Zazzle http://www.zazzle.com

Café Press http://www.cafepress.com

Elmer's Photo Patchwork https://itunes.apple.com/us/app/elmers-photo-patchwork/
id967262500?mt=8

Kuddle https://itunes.apple.com/us/app/kuddle/id901082502?mt=8

Priime https://itunes.apple.com/app/priime/id934587545?mt=8

FrameMagic https://itunes.apple.com/us/app/framemagic-all-in-one/id457447080? mt=8

Little Story Creator https://itunes.apple.com/us/app/little-story-creator-digital/id7217
82955?mt=8

Once students are comfortable with cameras, apps, and online editing, take the show on the road. Start a photography club, form an "Image Squad," and offer assistance to students and staff members who would like to polish their photography skills. Recruit local professionals to share their expertise with interested amateurs. Promote visual literacy whenever and however you can.

Activity 9: Digital Badges

Bloom's levels of cognitive learning: Apply, Analyze, Create

Digital badges are visible indicators of the acquisition of desired skills or knowledge. Like traditional scouting patches and military service emblems, digital badges tell the world that those who display them have reached a certain, measurable level of achievement. The badges can either be given as rewards or bestowed when specific criteria are met. Some colleges require students to complete a series of learning modules, with badges tracking their progress through the course material.

In 2013, the city of Chicago sponsored a Summer of Learning, inviting children and young adults to "Explore your city, earn badges, and level up your future." The initiative spawned a City of Learning movement that is now active in Pittsburgh, Columbus, Dallas, Los Angeles, and Washington, D.C., as well as in the founding city of Chicago. Badges remain an integral part of the program. Participants choose from programs hosted at local museums, libraries, and universities or earn their badges completely online.

The Smithsonian Institution offers online Smithsonian Quests designed to encourage discovery and collaboration. Once registered on the site, students work through a series of activities (including the creation of an artifact), with ongoing evaluation and coaching from the Smithsonian Educator Advisory Committee. Upon successful completion of a Quest, the student is awarded a digital badge to display on his/her own school account.

Digital badges can be a nice classroom incentive as well as a visual assessment tool. Rather than use premade badges, invite students to design original ones at 3D Badge Maker. Brainstorm a list of symbolic images that represent a desired skill (a pen and notebook for Writing; a magnifying glass for Research, etc.) Upload photos and add text to the button templates available on the Badge Maker site. Alternately, do a search for free icons at Iconfinder (put in a search term, then filter for "Free" under price) for images to use on the badges. The Shapes feature on the Frames page in PicMonkey will also allow students to edit and label original badges. This option is better for resizing and creating larger badges.

Save finished badges in an online folder, to be awarded by the teacher when students complete their badge requirements. Once badges have been earned, encourage students to showcase their learning by displaying badges on personal folders or blogs or by printing them out to exhibit in the classroom.

These two badges were made with badgemaker. The one on the left uses an image from iconfinder; the one on the right has an original uploaded photo for its background. "Badgemaker." (Photo by the author, Creative Commons license, some rights reserved. Retrieved from https://www.flickr.com/photos/dmcordell/16683056325.)

Variations

- Use Badge Maker to create genre signs for the library or classroom book collection. Print out the finished product as signs or stickers.

Make genre labels by using editing photos using PicMonkey's shape frames, then adding text. "Buttons Collage." (Photo by the author, Creative Commons license, some rights reserved. Retrieved from https://www.flickr.com/photos/dmcordell/16682041812.)

- Have students volunteer to create visual signage for special needs, ESL, or foreign language classrooms.

Resource Box 23

Chicago Summer of Learning http://www.chicagosummeroflearning.org

Cities of Learning http://citiesoflearning.org

Smithsonian Quests http://smithsonianquests.org

6 Reasons to Incorporate "Smithsonian Quests" into Your Classroom http://theinnovativeeducator.blogspot.com/2013/03/6-reasons-to-incorporate-smithsonian.html

Online Badge Maker http://www.onlinebadgemaker.com/3d-badge-maker

Iconfinder https://www.iconfinder.com

Activity 10: Here's My Card

Bloom's levels of cognitive learning: Apply, Analyze, Evaluate, Create

Business cards help create a memorable first impression. Introduce students to this staple of adult life by having them design a simple personal calling card.

Students will first need to take or scan a photo of themselves (this might be the perfect opportunity to initiate a discussion about digital footprint, appropriate self-portraits, and posting selfies). Next, they should be directed to select a quote that they feel expresses an important message or summarizes their philosophy of life. Sites like The Quotations Page, Brainy Quote, and The Quote Garden offer quotes arranged by author and topic. The Library Spot has links to additional sources of memorable sayings.

Using the design option on a photo-editing site like Ribbet, create a custom canvas (standard business card size of 3.5" x 2" easily translates to dimensions of

3500 x 2000). Upload the desired photo and position it on the screen. With the text option, add a chosen quote, experimenting with different sizes and fonts to achieve a pleasing composition. If the business cards will be saved and used online only, playing with colors and effects is fun. However, if the final product will be printed out (on cardstock or using commercial business card sheets), limiting both the photos and the text to black and white might be more cost effective.

Combine an inspirational quote with a self-portrait to represent how you see yourself and the world. "My Card." (Photo by the author, Creative Commons license, some rights reserved. Retrieved from https://www.flickr.com/photos/dmcordell/16496918189.)

Variations

- High school students might want to design and purchase actual business cards from a commercial site like Zazzle, which offers both templates and create-your-own options, to use at college and job interviews.

- Rather than photos of themselves, challenge students to use the photo of a place or artifact that represents them: their favorite piece of sports equipment, a view of the mountains where they like to hike, etc. Match the quote to the image.

- Instead of a personal card, have students make one for a famous person. Use public domain photos and search for actual quotes from the chosen figure.

Activity 11: Photo Cube

Bloom's levels of cognitive learning: Apply, Create

While many craft sites provide directions about how to decoupage photographs onto wooden blocks, Big Huge Labs offers an easy paper alternative. Select a maximum of six photos (from your computer or from Flickr). If fewer are chosen, the site will substitute plain colored squares on the empty sides. Once the images are uploaded, the tool creates a flat design that can be printed out and folded into a 3D object.

Have students design their cubes with a theme in mind. They might use the photo cubes to remember an event, present information, or tell a story. If text is to be included, either add it to the image during editing or write on the squares before the cube is folded together.

Variations

- Make greeting card cubes by selecting images with personal meaning for the recipient. Add a special message before assembling.

- Have individuals or groups make cubes, then challenge class members to guess the theme.

- Use the cubes as visual study aids. Find public domain images for a specific topic, create a cube, and let the pictures serve as memory jogs.

- Collect photographs that might serve as visual story starters and make them into photo cubes. Roll a cube and use the image that comes up on top as the inspiration for a written or verbal story.

Resource Box 24

The Quotations Page http://www.quotationspage.com

Brainy Quote http://www.brainyquote.com

The Quote Garden http://www.quotegarden.com

Library Spot http://www.libraryspot.com/quotations.htm

Big Huge Labs Photocube http://bighugelabs.com/cube.php

Activity 12: Reports and Presentations

Bloom's levels of cognitive learning: Understand, Apply, Analyze, Evaluate, Create

Organizing and presenting ideas is a valuable life skill that students should begin practicing from an early age. There are a number of ways in which photographs can be used to effectively convey content:

- Aurasma: This free app utilizes *augmented reality* (AR is a view of the real-world environment enhanced with computer-generated sound, video, or graphics) to add interactivity to images. An "aura" is data—video, web link, or animation—attached to an image, object, or place. As an example, students could take photos of their classroom projects, print these photos, and link the image to a short video in which they explain their product. Any viewer with access to a mobile device that has the Aurasma app installed would then be able to view the auras. Interactive journals, enhanced book reports, and living art/photography galleries (with students discussing what they've created) are among the possibilities available through AR.

- Quick Response (QR) Codes: An early form of AR, these matrix barcodes can be read by an imaging device (most commonly a smartphone, tablet, or computer camera). When scanned, the QR code links to a website or text documents. Students have used QR codes to access book reviews, images, wikis, or school reports, and to follow the clues on scavenger hunts. Some teachers provide QR codes on Parent Nights, to provide easy access to information.

Students use QR code readers to follow the clues on a field trip scavenger hunt. "QR Code Clue Card—CLUE 3 of 6—A6." (Photo by Roy Blumenthal , Creative Commons license, some rights reserved. Retrieved from flickr.com/photos/royblumenthal/6102201515.)

- Thinglink: This tool allows students to create interactive posters, maps, and albums by using photos and other images as connectors to information. When a mouse scrolls over the selected image, a "tag" opens with text, a link, even a video clip. Thinglinks provide an engaging format for students to share reports on books, historical figures, current events, or almost any curricular topic.

- Animoto: Users upload photos, select background music, and let the site create a short video with music and effects. Students can create Animotos to promote school events, share projects, or highlight their classroom activities. (See also Activity 10, Digital Storytelling.)

*A Note about "Death by PowerPoint"

PowerPoint is just a tool, inherently neither good nor bad. It is how the tool is *used* that makes the difference. "Death by PowerPoint" is a phrase that describes the results of the poor application of presentation software by a speaker, the "death" being the sense of boredom and emotional disconnect felt by his/her audience.

Many educators have been subjected to professional development training that includes text-heavy slideshows. Some presenters even distribute handouts that are merely printouts of the slides. As we prepare students for life beyond the classroom, it is important to give them practice in constructing and delivering information in a compelling manner.

Utilizing some of the previously mentioned tools, like Animoto or Thinglink, is one way to add visual elements to a presentation. Even PowerPoint slideshows gain impact when images predominate and text is kept to a minimum. Author, speaker, and graphic design guru Guy Kawasaki preaches the 10-20-30 rule: a maximum of ten slides, presented in twenty minutes, with thirty-point (fairly large) font. Bullet points, particularly those read to the audience by the speaker, are considered anathema. While Kawasaki's strictures may seem extreme, they do provide a template for more streamlined narratives.

Another presentation model is an Ignite event. Participants must use twenty slides, with each slide advancing automatically after fifteen seconds, for a total of five minutes speaking time. These quick bursts of information are meant to "ignite" the audience's passion for an idea. Longer in duration, but uniquely compelling, are the TED (Technology, Entertainment, Design) Talks. The TED mission is to offer a platform for "the world's most inspired thinkers" by sponsoring public events and freely sharing videos of the talks. Select a TED Talk to share with students. Have them evaluate design as well as content, paying particular attention to the graphics chosen to help convey the speaker's message.

Ask each student to prepare a short PowerPoint about a personal passion, but specify that they may only use text on the title slide and for any citations. Stress that images must complement their spoken commentary. As an added challenge, let volunteers attempt a TED-style, 10-20-30, or Ignite presentation. Request a spot at the next school board meeting for a few students to share their presentations.

Resource Box 25

Aurasma http://www.aurasma.com/aura

Meaningful Integration of Augmented Reality in Education http://www.twoguysandsomeipads.com/p/meaningful-integration.html

40 Interesting Ways to Use QR Codes in the Classroom (pdf) http://aftech.pbworks.com/f/40_Interesting_Ways_to_Use_QR_Codes_in_the_Cla%281%29.pdf

Twelve Ideas for Teaching with QR Codes http://www.edutopia.org/blog/QR-codes-teaching-andrew-miller

ThingLink https://www.thinglink.com

Animoto http://animoto.com/#examples

Guy Kawasaki 10-20-30 Rule http://guykawasaki.com/the_102030_rule

Ignite http://igniteshow.com

TED Talks https://www.ted.com/talks

Curating and Sharing Images

Standards addressed:

- Common Core State Standards: CCSS.ELA-Literacy.CCRA.SL.5

- AASL Standards for the 21st Century Learner: 3.1.2, 3.1.4
- ISTE Standards for Students: 2a, 2b, 2c, 2d

Essential Questions:

- What is the value of curating?
- In what ways does photography influence society?
- Do photographers have a responsibility to society?
- How can photography connect a community?
- How do digital images preserve history?

Activity 1: What Is Curation?

Bloom's levels of cognitive learning: Understand, Apply, Analyze, Evaluate

Students may not be familiar with the term *curation* as it is used to describe the gathering, sorting, arranging, and sharing of content.

Start a discussion by asking if anyone in the class has a collection. Solicit details about what they collect, how they choose new items to add, and how they arrange and store the items in the collection. Relate this collecting activity to museums, which are themed collections of "stuff," managed by curators.

This carefully chosen gallery of images relates the history of a stately mansion in Vermont. "History of Yester House." (Photo by the author, Creative Commons license, some rights reserved. Retrieved from http://flickr.com/photos/dmcordell/16595240407.)

Now visit a museum site, like the National Gallery of Art. Note that the collection is divided into sections, including paintings, sculptures, and photographs, and that information is attached to individual items, identifying medium, artist, title, year of creation, and more. Discuss why it is important not only to *collect* pieces but also to make them *usable* and *accessible*.

Keeping in mind a collection they have or would like to have, direct students (1) to write a vision statement describing the focus and purpose of their collection and (2) to draw up a list of questions that they, as curators, might ask before adding a new artifact. Have them also include ideas about how to share their collections with others.

Activity 2: Curate an Exhibit

Bloom's levels of cognitive learning: Understand, Apply, Analyze, Evaluate, Create

Curating is not just collecting similar items, although that is part of it. Curation can also serve the larger goal of benefiting other users in their search for information and resources. When selecting, arranging, and tagging curated images, students use critical thinking skills; in sharing the images, they also refine collaboration and communication skills.

In order to have value and meaning, collected images need to be sorted, arranged, and tagged or labeled. "Photo Archives, The Free Library of Philadelphia." (Photo by the author, Creative Commons license, some rights reserved. Retrieved from http://flickr.com/photos/dmcordell/16801416831.)

Begin by giving students a better idea of the curation process. Visit the CoTA (Collaborations: Teachers and Artists) site and review the steps in "How to Curate a Museum Exhibition." Following these guidelines, have students design an online photography exhibit, perhaps using some of the images they have captured in a photowalk or makerspace activity. Discuss how the exhibit might be shared: as a Flickr album, on Tumblr, via a page on the school website, etc. If the still photos are combined into a slideshow, they might also be uploaded as a YouTube video or Animoto slideshow.

While receiving feedback is very empowering, the teacher should monitor social networking sites and consider disabling comments should anything inappropriate appear. Curated exhibits could also be shared with students in another classroom or district who have done a similar activity.

Variations

- Children's Rooms in some public libraries have designated spaces where young patrons display their personal collections. If your classroom does not have a case available for use, set up an exhibition area on a shelf or the top of a bookcase. Require student curators to write a description to include in the exhibit. Take photos of the curators with their collections and make a catalog/album with tags and identifying information.

- As a culminating senior project, have each student curate an exhibit highlighting his/her school years. The process should include selection, evaluation, and tagging of artifacts, including images that represent meaningful, powerful, or memorable learning experiences. To add impact, incorporate all of the exhibits into a Museum of the Class of ____ and invite family members to visit.

- Play the Curation Game. View an online collection of photographs, for example, the Commons on Flickr (see Activity 6, Copyright and Fair Use, for more public domain sites). Invite students to select an image for a curated exhibit. They must then write a description, explain their interpretation of the work, and add some identifying tags. The "exhibit" may be printed out and hung in the classroom or saved and displayed virtually.

Adding tags to a photo make it easier to find, both for the creator and for other image searchers. "Tagging." (Photo by the author, Creative Commons license, some rights reserved. Retrieved from http://flickr.com/photos/dmcordell/15250410618.)

Activity 3: Tagging

Bloom's levels of cognitive learning: Understand, Apply, Analyze, Evaluate

It is important that students understand the necessity of adding keywords (tags) to their digital content so that it can be organized, searched, and retrieved. Instruct students to read the Search Tips page at Pics4Learning, then practice finding images appropriate for specific school projects. Have them list the words or phrases they used and which yielded the best results.

Next, display an image from a photo-hosting site like Flickr and ask students to brainstorm possible keywords. Compare the students' list with the actual tags used by the photographer. Decide why certain tags were selected and whether the students agree with the choices.

Variation

Students who use social networking sites are familiar with hashtags, words or phrases preceded by the # symbol. Hashtags allow for the grouping of comments on a specific topic and are searchable.

Each year, cultural organizations from around the world participate in Museum Week, which is designed to encourage interest in the arts. In March 2015, the public was invited to contribute to #MuseumWeek daily themes via hashtags, including #souvenirsMW (sharing memories of museums and art, including photographs), #architectureMW (images of the institutions and their surrounding landscapes), and #poseMW (taking selfies in galleries and museums).

Older students could, of course, participate in the actual Museum Week events. Create a similar activity for a school event, like Spirit Week. Have students take photos with specific themes on designated days. Save the images to a Flickr album, using the hashtags as photo tags so that they can be searched by theme. If your district will allow teachers to access Twitter during class time, demonstrate how a hashtag search would work. Searching #tlchat (teacher librarian chat) or #edchat (education chat) will bring school-appropriate results.

Activity 4: Create a Virtual Bulletin Board

Bloom's levels of cognitive learning: Apply, Analyze, Evaluate, Create

Bulletin boards are visual by nature. Challenge students to convey a message or represent a theme solely in images. While this activity could be done with printed photos on a physical board, students might enjoy trying out Padlet, a collaborative site that allows the addition of content (text, images, links, and video clips) to a "wall" by anyone with the unique address created for the owner. Padlet is free to use, but walls can only be saved if the user registers for an account. An alternative would be to take a screenshot of the completed padlet. Padlet is also useful for curating resources for research projects.

Resource Box 26

National Gallery of Art http://www.nga.gov/content/ngaweb/Collection.html

The Commons on Flickr https://www.flickr.com/commons

Curating for Education (wiki) http://curatingisthecure.wikispaces.com

How to Curate a Museum Exhibition http://cotaprogram.org/how-tos/how-to-curate-a-museum-exhibition

18 Ways to Use Flickr in Schools http://www.colourmylearning.com/2013/03/flickr-for-education-18-ways-to-use-flickr-in-schools

Introduction to Using Tumblr in the Classroom https://www.avemariapress.com/engagingfaith/2011/11/introduction-using-tumblr-classroom

Pics4Learning http://www.pics4learning.com

#MuseumWeek http://mashable.com/2015/03/22/museumweek-2015

Padlet http://padlet.com

Technology Resource Teachers: Padlet http://education.fcps.org/trt/padlet

---

Variation

Create a "What Is the Question?" padlet. Display a photo in the center that is the "answer" (e.g., a portrait of Helen Keller). Have students do some research on the answer topic, then post appropriate questions: "Whom did Annie Sullivan teach?" "What world famous writer and lecturer could not see or hear."

Activity 5: Connecting with the Past

Bloom's levels of cognitive learning: Understand, Apply, Create

Historypin calls itself "A global community collaborating around history." It is a digital archive of historical photos, videos, audio recordings, and personal recollections submitted and annotated by users, who log in with Google, Facebook, or Twitter accounts. Have students access the Projects page to see the collections, then click on the map to see more information about individual photos. Discuss how students might create an annotated map with their own photos and what its focus might be. If brainstorming yields a unique theme, submit it to the website and Historypin will consider adding it to their Projects page.

A similar site is What Was There, which ties historical photos to Google maps. Free registration is required to upload photos, but it is possible to search the maps by city, state, or country without registering. All photos are tagged with location and date.

Other sites where students can create visual timelines for free are Timetoast and timeline.

Resource Box 27

History Pin https://www.historypin.org/

What Was There http://www.whatwasthere.com/default.aspx

Timetoast http://www.timetoast.com

Timeline http://www.readwritethink.org/files/resources/interactives/timeline_2

Activity 6: It's a Small World

Bloom's levels of cognitive learning: Understand, Apply, Analyze, Create

Making connections, engaging in collaborative tasks, and effectively communicating ideas are all key life skills. Video conferencing platforms like Skype (free, registration required) and Google Hangouts (free, Google Account required) provide the means for students to interact with their peers from around the state, around the country, and around the world. Projects can be tied to almost any curricular area, from science to social studies to English language arts, adding authenticity and engagement to learning units. Working together with classes in other cultures on projects that incorporate digital images is a powerful way to foster a spirit of global community.

Note: A little prep work is necessary to be successful with this type of activity:

- Check with your IT (Information Technology) department to be sure that Skype, Hangouts, or any similar platform you wish to use is not blocked in your district.

- If your preferred site is not available, ask IT for an alternative method by which to make the connection.

- Decide if you will use a computer or large screen for the chat and have all equipment set up in advance.

- Do a test run with your remote partner teacher to be sure that everything works.

- Be mindful of time zones when you plan, especially if you're connecting with a class in another state or country.

- Discuss the procedure with your students. If this is their first video chat, role-play in advance, perhaps selecting one representative to introduce the class and welcome virtual guests.

Variations

- Instaweather: A spin-off of the wildly popular Instagram, this iPhone/iPad app, available in both free and pro versions, attaches geographic location, temperature, date, and time to a digital image. Take an Instaweather photo or series of photos across a designated time span (students could be in charge of snapping the morning weather, for example). Compare and contrast seasons and climate with partner classrooms in other cities, states, or countries.

- Flat Stanley: Many classes already participate in this type of activity, where paper people are exchanged and photographed in various locations. Expand on the concept by sending actual photos of students rather than drawings. Or change the project to Selfie Stanley: students take selfies of themselves near local landmarks, gather the photos into a folder or Flickr album, and share the photo sets with other classes. During a follow-up video call, students explain where the selfie was taken and why they chose that particular location.

- Shelfies: In many ways, we are what we read. Shelfies are selfies taken in front of a bookshelf or bookcase; the photographers typically hold a favorite title in their hands. Invite students to share their reading choices with others; see which titles have universal appeal and which are more popular in a specific area or country.

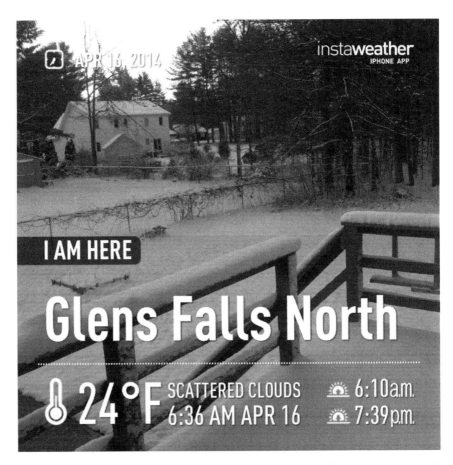

Compare weather data with students in other parts of the world. "April Snow Event." (Photo by the author, Creative Commons license, some rights reserved. Retrieved from http://flickr.com/photos/dmcordell/13902517144.)

- Toy Stories: You can learn a lot about people from the objects they value. Photographer Gabriele Galimberti spent more than two years documenting what boys and girls in 58 countries consider their most prized possessions. Ask students to photograph their favorite playthings. Exchange and discuss these images with children in other locales.

- What the World Eats: Have students take photos of school lunches or holiday meals to compare with those of their peers in different states or countries.

- International Dot Day: Inspired by Peter Reynolds's book *The Dot*, teacher Terry Shay instituted this celebration of creativity that now includes more than a million participants from 61 countries. Students make "dots" of all shapes, sizes, and materials, then share them with others via videoconferencing. Available teacher resources include a Google Document, to help plan classroom connections, and an Educator's Handbook with suggestions and tools, including activities created by Reynolds himself.

Take photos of paper people in front of local landmarks, then mail or scan and share with partner classes. "Flat Eric." (Photo by the author, Creative Commons license, some rights reserved. Retrieved from http://flickr.com/photos/dmcordell/5036997934.)

In the southern United States, eating Hoppin' John on New Year's Day is thought to bring a prosperous year filled with luck. "Our Lucky Supper." (Photo by the author, Creative Commons license, some rights reserved. Retrieved from http://flickr.com/photos/dmcordell/11694219815.)

Students from around the world celebrate creativity by decorating with dots. "International Dot Day." (Photo by the author, Creative Commons license, some rights reserved. Retrieved from https://www.flickr.com/photos/dmcordell/16063105403.)

Activity 7: Text(book) It

Bloom's levels of cognitive learning: Understand, Apply, Analyze, Create

Rather than doing reports that are just summations of other people's work, challenge your students to curate a visual textbook. Have them start by gathering information about a specific topic, perhaps the history of their town. After they have finished the initial research, students should collaborate to create a story outline. Assign photographers to take photos of landmarks; add downloaded vintage images obtained from public domain sources (see Activity 6, Copyright and Fair Use) or local historical societies. Evaluate the images to select ones that will fit the narrative. Sort, arrange, and label all artifacts. Add text to the images and print out the final product. Create an online version as a Flickr album, with text displayed below the photo title.

Since sharing information is an important part of curation, make print copies of the book available in the school and community. On Flickr, use tags so that others can find the album when doing a keyword search.

Two apps that can be used for creating books are the following:

- Book Creator: a paid app that creates e-books that can be e-mailed, printed, and uploaded to the iBooks store for purchase or free download. Authors can add images, videos, music, and voice-overs.

- iBooks Author: free app or Mac download that allows users to create books for iPads and Macs. Use templates or customize with images, text, and interactive elements. Also allows for uploads to the iBooks store.

Activity 8: Where Do I Keep It?

Bloom's levels of cognitive learning: Understand, Apply, Analyze, Evaluate, Create

Curation refers to the gathering, organizing, and storing of content. If student products are designed to be authentic, with value in the "real" (non-school) world, then some thought should be given to archiving representative works. With the prevalence of digital photography, images of family, friends, and daily life that aren't archived somewhere will be lost to succeeding generations.

Many photographers choose Flickr as their storage site. Even if students are too young to have their own accounts, consider setting up a class account under a teacher's name. Explain the value of tagging (adding keywords) so that specific photos can be located. Discuss what albums are and how they can be used to arrange images that have the same theme. Review other features, like geotagging (adding the photo to a map), licensing (Flickr photos are automatically copyright protected but the owner can choose to give them Creative Commons licensing), and viewing options (Private, Public, or shared only with Family or Friends). Try searching for images that other people have uploaded to Flickr (go to the Advanced Search page to make sure that SafeSearch is turned on).

The Library of Congress, along with other libraries and museums around the world, has uploaded images to a special section of Flickr called The Commons. Visitors to the site are asked to "Please help make the photographs you enjoy more discoverable by adding tags and leaving comments. Your contributions and

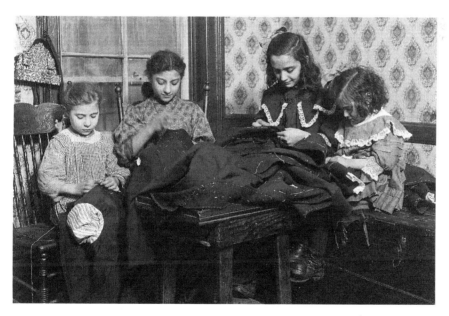

The Commons, on Flickr, shares copyright-friendly archival images from a number of libraries and museums. "Garment Workers. Katrina De Cato, 6 years old, Franco Brezoo, 11 years old, Maria Attreo, 12 years old, Mattie Attreo, 5 years old. 4 P.M. New York City, January 1910." (Photo by Lewis Hine, U.S. National Archives' Local Identifier: 102-LH-1309, no known copyright restrictions. Retrieved from https://www.flickr.com/photos/usnationalarchives/7496206456.)

knowledge make these photos even richer." Thus, The Commons provides both interactivity and authenticity as students explore the rich content and provide additional content for what they view.

Once students understand curation basics, show them a few other options:

- The Library of Congress personal archiving page provides tips on scanning and preserving images.

- Pinterest serves as a visual bulletin board for collecting and displaying resources. Users can create an account via their e-mail address or by connecting to Facebook or Twitter. In addition to "pinning" content from the Internet, it is possible to use a Share button to pin Flickr images to Pinterest, where they can be arranged on topic boards and tagged.

Activity 9: Where Do I Keep It #2: Portfolios

Bloom's levels of cognitive learning: Understand, Apply, Analyze, Evaluate, Create

Portfolios are useful as both assessment tools and archival collection sites. Students should be expected to reflect upon their work and select for inclusion the products most representative of their growth as a learner. The artifacts stored in the portfolio can be used to showcase an individual's accomplishments as he or she moves beyond the K–12 classroom and into higher education or the workplace.

Before exploring portfolio options, take time to discuss the purpose and scope of this type of curating with students. Make expectations about the quality and quantity of content clear from the beginning. Explain when and how teachers will access the portfolios as part of ongoing learning assessment.

Some possibilities for student portfolios include the following:

1. Apps

    - Evernote: productivity software that can be downloaded on a Mac computer or added as an app on iPhones and iPads. With Evernote, students can capture photos, take notes, record audio, and make entries searchable. Its ease of use makes Evernote a popular digital portfolio option in classrooms.

    - Portfolium: allows users to create a visual portfolio by uploading photos and arranging them by topic. This app is promoted as being appropriate for academic and business use, so it could serve a student beyond high school.

    - Seesaw: a digital portfolio app where students can add and annotate photos of their work. Also supports text, video, and audio. It is possible for parents to create accounts that allow them to see what their children have added to a portfolio. Recommended for students as young as five years old via class accounts.

2. Platforms and tools

    - Tackk: a site for creating blogs, web pages and portfolios. Students can log in by opening an account or via a variety of sites, including

Edmodo. It is possible to archive reports and projects, with images and videos, and share resources via social networking options.

- Flavors Me: a tool that will help students create a website to store images, audio, and video.

- Blog: a platform where users can share written postings and images. Kid-Blog and Edublogs are two of the best-known blogging sites for students.

Resource Box 29

7 Things You Should Know about Flickr http://net.educause.edu/ir/library/pdf/ELI7034.pdf

The Commons (Flickr) https://www.flickr.com/commons

About SlideShare http://www.slideshare.net/about

Library of Congress, Personal Archiving: Preserving Your Digital Memories http://www.digitalpreservation.gov/personalarchiving/index.html

How to Use Pinterest http://www.realsimple.com/work-life/technology/how-to-use-pinterest-00100000087471

Using Pinterest in Education (a Pinterest board) http://www.pinterest.com/twahlert/using-pinterest-in-education

Evernote http://evernote.com/evernote

Evernote App (iPhones and iPads) https://itunes.apple.com/us/app/evernote/id281796108?mt=8

Portfolium https://portfolium.com

Seesaw https://itunes.apple.com/us/app/seesaw-multimedia-journal/id930565184

Seesaw—Students Build Digital Portfolios on Their iPads http://www.freetech4teachers.com/2015/01/seesaw-students-build-digital.html#.VQhqyGb5_V0

Tackk https://tackk.com

How to Use Tackk to Create Blogs and Digital Portfolios http://www.freetech4teachers.com/2015/02/how-to-use-tackk-to-create-blogs-and.html

Flavors Me https://flavors.me

Kidblog http://kidblog.org/home

Edublogs http://edublogs.org

Digital Storytelling

Standards addressed:

- Common Core State Standards: CCSS.ELA-Literacy.CCRA.SL.2
- AASL Standards for the 21st Century Learner: 4.1.3, 4.1.8
- ISTE Standards for Students: 1a, 1b

Essential Questions:

- What is the role of stories in people's lives?
- What do stories tell people about themselves?
- How can photography connect a community?
- How do digital images preserve history?

Activity 1: Portrait of Our Community

Bloom's levels of cognitive learning: Apply, Analyze, Create

Humans of New York (HONY) is a project launched by photographer Brandon Stanton in November 2010. Stanton collected over 6,000 street portraits and interviews in New York City, sharing them on a blog and, later, in a book. In addition to providing a fascinating glimpse of ordinary lives, HONY has also spearheaded some successful charity drives, including one to aid the victims of Hurricane Sandy.

Take some time as a class to explore the photos on the Humans of New York site. Have students decide which portraits they like and analyze their appeal: is it the physical characteristics of the person captured, the effectiveness of the shot, the quote displayed with the photo, or some combination of the three? Following Stanton's model, ask students to either take a photograph of a family or other community member (with permission, of course) or find an existing photo, and request that the person in the picture provide a short response to a predetermined question, for example, "What are you most proud of in your life?" Brainstorming a list of possible interview questions would be the perfect lead-in to this project. The resulting Humans of Our Community collection might be displayed in a gallery, posted on a bulletin board, or used to create a book. This type of activity could easily be turned into a service project done in partnership with a local senior center or nursing home (see Activity 1, Curating and Sharing Images).

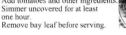

"Recipe Card Template." (Photo by the author, Creative Commons license, some rights reserved. Retrieved from https://www.flickr.com/photos/dmcordell/16060790984.)

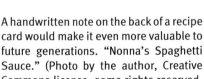

A handwritten note on the back of a recipe card would make it even more valuable to future generations. "Nonna's Spaghetti Sauce." (Photo by the author, Creative Commons license, some rights reserved. Retrieved from https://www.flickr.com/photos/dmcordell/16495731140.)

Activity 2: A Taste of Home

Bloom's levels of cognitive learning: Apply, Analyze, Create

The sharing of a meal is an important bonding experience; documenting family recipes helps to preserve and strengthen generational ties.

Have students take photos of one of their favorite home-cooked foods. Using an editing site like Ribbet, start with a blank canvas and create a simple recipe template. Use the text option to add cooking directions, and insert a photo to illustrate the finished dish. Or, print out some recipe card templates, add text by hand, and attach printouts of the photos. Finished recipes could be incorporated into a cookbook or printed out individually for display.

Extension Activities

- Collaborate with the Home and Careers teacher to have students actually cook the recipes and hold a tasting.

- Take a photo of a family member holding the cooked item and interview him/her about personal memories attached to the dish. Have him/her add hand-written comments on the back of the recipe card.

- Ask students to classify and tag recipes by course (entrée, dessert, beverage), country of origin, or other key words (quick & easy; one-pot meals, holidays, etc.).

Resource Box 30

Humans of New York http://www.humansofnewyork.com

Step-by-Step Guide to Oral History http://dohistory.org/on_your_own/toolkit/oral History.html

Tell Me Your Stories (project ideas) http://www.tellmeyourstories.org/sample

The Power of Food and the Importance of Family Recipes http://www.street directory.com/food_editorials/cooking/recipes/the_power_of_food_and_the_importance _of_family_recipes.html

My Family Traditions: A Class Book and a Potluck Lunch http://www.readwrite think.org/classroom-resources/lesson-plans/family-traditions-class-book-941.html

---

Activity 3: What Are They Saying?

Bloom's levels of cognitive learning: Apply, Analyze, Evaluate, Create

Writers of historical fiction frequently invent conversations that *might* have taken place, based on the personalities of the people involved and the environment in which they lived. Author Michael Frayn believes "The great challenge is to get inside people's heads, to stand where they stood and see the world as they saw it, to make some informed estimate of their motives and intentions. The only way into the protagonists' heads is through the imagination."

Challenge students to imagine what a famous person, fictional character, or even an inanimate object or animal might say, then literally put words in their mouths by using an editing tool to insert speech bubbles. One easy-to-use site is Speechable, where users can upload an image, add a bubble and text, then save and share the finished product. PhraseIt offers similar options.

Variations

- For biography projects, direct students to download a copyright-friendly image of their person and then attach a speech bubble with the person's name and the reason why he/she is famous or what that person might say if alive today.

What would Lincoln say? "Abraham Lincoln (phrase.it)." (Photo by the author, Creative Commons license, some rights reserved. Retrieved from https://www.flickr.com/photos/dmcordell/15261853395.)

- Upload photos of family pets and try to imagine how they might express themselves if they could talk. Record their "comments" in a speech bubble.

- Some teachers end a class by requiring students to submit a reflection, question, or brief summation, an "exit ticket." Have students add speech bubbles to images to serve as a visual record of what they've learned.

If cats could talk . . . "Gretel." (Photo by the author, Creative Commons license, some rights reserved. Retrieved from https://www.flickr.com/photos/dmcordell/16657142846.)

Activity 4: Adding Voices

Bloom's levels of cognitive learning: Apply, Analyze, Evaluate, Create

Every person has a story to tell. The collected stories of a nation compose its history. It is important to record first-person testimony from accounts of world-changing events (World War II, the JFK assassination, September 11 attacks) to reminiscences about daily life as it used to be lived before the memories fade and are lost. Adding spoken commentary to photographs greatly increases the significance of the images, helping to preserve community and personal histories. Speech adds a human element sometimes lacking in text alone.

One way to blend photos with voice is though Fotobabble, where it is possible to add narrative to an uploaded image. Let students create primary source artifacts by photographing a relative or neighbor, then having the person in the photo speak about a remembered historic event. Alternately, students could ask the interviewees to provide their own vintage photographs for scanning, then record the memories attached to the image. To add a deeper level of authenticity to the project, encourage students to request permission to share the products they create with a local historical society. Where appropriate, such reminiscences might be also submitted to the Library of Congress Veterans History Project and similar oral history databases.

Variations

- Have students introduce themselves to classmates by making a Fotobabble with information about a hobby or favorite possession.

- Make a Fotobabble album after a field trip or photowalk, with students commenting on the images they have collected.

- Use Fotobabble as part of an ethnic heritage activity. Students upload photos of something representative of their family culture, then explain what this object means to them.

- In a foreign language (or ESL) class, students collaborate to create a "speaking" dictionary of terms, labeling the images of common objects in both English and another language.

- Rather than transport objects from home for a show-and-tell activity, students display photos with recorded commentary about why they chose a particular item to share.

- For added fun, try Blabberize, where it is possible to add mouth movement to photos.

Create talking images with mouths that move. "Sea Lion (Blabberize screenshot)." (Photo by the author, Creative Commons license, some rights reserved. Retrieved from https://www.flickr.com/photos/dmcordell/16495662310.)

Activity 5: Time Travel

Bloom's levels of cognitive learning: Analyze, Apply, Create

A time capsule is a container, holding artifacts representative of a specific people or place that is meant to be opened at a future date. Such a cache of goods and information is intended to convey a "snapshot" of a moment in time once the contents of the capsule are revealed. Photographs, properly dated and identified, are a wonderful way to visually explain an era. Time capsules can be as simple as a shoebox or as sophisticated as a metal tube encased in cement.

Before beginning a time capsule project, lay the groundwork. Look at vintage yearbooks or photo albums and ask students what they would like to know about life in the "old days," then imagine what future generations might want to know about life today. Brainstorm lists of possible items to incorporate, including images of popular sports, foods, clothing, hairstyles, and community hangouts. Take a group shot of the students assembling the time capsule and include it with the other artifacts. Finally, decide where the capsule should be stored and when it should be opened.

Variations

Send a message to the future with a time capsule. "Time Capsule Project." (Photo by woodleywonderworks, Creative Commons license, some rights reserved. Retrieved from https://www.flickr.com/photos/wwworks/3164910901.)

- Assemble the time capsule during the first week of school. In addition to photos, and small personal mementos, include a sheet that each student fills out titled "About Me." Open the capsule on the last day of the school year, review information, and celebrate positive changes.

- Challenge older students to travel back in time, to create a time capsule for a specific decade using public domain images. For example, a 1960s collection could include news photos of the Kennedy assassination, images of hippies at Woodstock, and a photo of the early Beatles. Viewers should be able to identify the decade by the images it generated. An extension of this concept could be for students to decide which decade they would most like to visit based on the photos in the different time capsules.

- Go in the other direction—move forward in time. Have students use an editing site to transform themselves into citizens of the future. Include altered buildings, food, and other items in the "message from the future" capsule.

- Instead of collecting items in a capsule, turn a photo into an interactive experience. Let students explore Indiana University's digital panorama, "In Mrs. Goldberg's Kitchen," the re-creation of a room in a Jewish family's early-20th- century home. Use thinglink (see Activity 8, Creating and Editing Images) to similarly enhance the uploaded photo of a classroom, locker, bedroom, or any other scene, adding explanatory text, links, videos, or audios.

Activity 6: Me Collage

Bloom's levels of cognitive learning: Apply, Analyze, Evaluate, Create

What we wear, how we decorate our spaces, even the pets we choose, reveal a lot of our personal story. Ask students to create a photo collage that visually expresses who they are or who they would like to become. Remind them that placement, color, text, and subject selection will all contribute to their unique version of a selfie.

Variations

- Hide the identity of the person who created the collage and ask classmates to guess the creator solely from the images used.

The contents of a shelf can tell a lot about the person who owns and stocks it. "Shelfie." (Photo by the author, Creative Commons license, some rights reserved. Retrieved from https://www.flickr.com/photos/dmcordell/16657294956.)

"Where I Read." (Photo by the author, Creative Commons license, some rights reserved. Retrieved from https://www.flickr.com/photos/dmcordell/16495621638.)

- Hurst College Senior School Library sponsors a "Match the Shelfie to the Selfie" contest. Teachers provide both selfies (self-portraits) and shelfies (a photo of their bookshelves); entrants are challenged to correctly pair the photos by analyzing the shelf contents.

- Some libraries promote a "Where I Read" activity. Contributors take, or have a friend take, a photo of themselves reading books in a variety of places: in a boat, sitting on a tractor, even bouncing on a trampoline. This type of activity promotes not only storytelling but also reading. Placing the photos on a map adds additional interest.

Activity 7: What's in Your Backpack?

Bloom's levels of cognitive learning: Apply, Analyze, Create

"The Contents of My Backpack." (Photo by Andrew Allingham, Creative Commons license, some rights reserved. Retrieved from https://www.flickr.com/photos/aallingh/ 5428801661.)

In *The Things They Carried*, author Tim O'Brien catalogs the "things," both tangible (letters, photos) and intangible (emotions, memories), that soldiers brought with them into battle. "They carried all they could bear, and then some, including a silent awe for the terrible power of the things they carried."

"There's a sense of identity that people associate with their belongings," photographer Jason Travis says. "What's in your purse or your pocket or your backpack can represent something much larger." His Persona project features the portrait of an individual alongside a tabletop view of the contents of that person's bag, neatly organized.

After viewing samples of Travis's work, invite students to arrange and then photograph the contents of their backpack or tote bag. (It might be prudent to offer students the option to take the photos at home, rather than in a more public venue like a classroom). Ask them to explain what some of the items mean to them: what are the stories attached to the artifacts? Browse the collection of images to compare and contrast what individuals consider necessities.

Variations

- Do a similar "What's in Your Locker" exercise.

- Make the project a collaborative one, involving a few different grade levels. Photograph and compare the items carried in school bags by elementary, middle, and high school students. Either request that parents help the younger children photograph the contents of their backpacks at home, or obtain parental permission for older students to assist the smaller ones in taking their own photos in the classroom.

- Flip the activity and have students decide what a well-equipped backpack should contain. What "essential" personal and educational items would they want to carry with them during the school day, for a trip, on a weekend?

Activity 8: Then and Now

Bloom's levels of cognitive learning: Apply, Analyze, Create

High school yearbook shots of celebrities and "Where Are They Now?" galleries of child stars are entertaining to view. Some siblings have posted images online of adult older brothers and sisters with their equally adult, and sometimes larger, younger sibs in their laps, in direct imitation of their baby photos. One mother

The comparison of a 1907 postcard image (top) with a photo taken in 2008 (bottom) shows only minor change in this Saratoga, New York, landmark. "Spit and Spat, Then and Now: 1907/2008." (Bottom photo by the author, Creative Commons license, some rights reserved. Retrieved from https://www.flickr.com/photos/dmcordell/16683344095. Original image [top] "CanfieldsPark2" by parkerdr, scanned postcard dated 1907, licensed under public domain via Wikimedia Commons. Retrieved from http://commons. wikimedia.org/wiki/File:CanfieldsPark2.JPG#mediaviewer/File: CanfieldsPark2.JPG.)

shared side-by-side photographs of her son on his first day of kindergarten and his first day of school as a high school senior.

Invite students to re-create old family photos. Have them sort through vintage pictures to find and scan a few with appropriate subject matter. The images could include the student as a child with a favorite toy, informal classroom photos from earlier grades, or a snapshot of an older pet as a young animal. Replicate the pose and props as closely as possible, with the teacher or fellow students capturing the results.

Alternately, this could be a family project, with the actual photos taken at home and later shared in the classroom. The collage option on an editing site can pair the photos and add explanatory text. Post the "Then and Now" photos on a bulletin board, present them as a special holiday gift, or include them in a class yearbook.

Variations

- Collect baby photos of staff members and have students guess their identities.

- Match vintage photos of scenes or buildings with modern photos of the same location. Display the images side by side or layer the new photo over the old one.

Layering vintage images over modern ones produces a fascinating contrast. "Merging Past and Present: 20th-Century Pennsylvania Avenue." (Photo by KamrenB Photography, Creative Commons license, some rights reserved. Retrieved from http://flickr.com/photos/kamgtr/14068367330.)

Activity 9: Memories

Bloom's levels of cognitive learning: Apply, Create

Since the early 19th century, traditional sewn memory quilts have been a popular way to document family history, pay tribute to the life of a loved one, or celebrate

A fiftieth wedding anniversary is commemorated in fabric and photos. "Memory Quilt." (Photo by Chhavi Creates, Creative Commons license, some rights reserved. Retrieved from http://flickr.com/photos/chhavicreates/6815550467.)

a milestone event. A modern twist on this concept is the photo quilt, which incorporates images of key people and events.

Construct a paper version of a photo quilt by gathering a set of related images that tell a story or represent a theme. Add a decorative border on an editing site, then print; or print the photos first and place them in construction paper frames. Tape the individual pieces together to form the quilt.

Variations

- Plan a paper Poetry Quilt for National Poetry Month (sponsored by the Academy of American Poets each April). Alternate blocks printed with the text of favorite poems and public domain images of their authors.

- Transfer selected images to fabric, then assemble and sew a quilt. This type of project might be done collaboratively with the Home and Careers teacher or as a community project with parent or senior citizen volunteers.

- Design completely virtual quilts using the collage option on PicMonkey, Ribbet, or Big Huge Labs to display in a slideshow. Alternately, create the collage/quilt online and print.

Resource Box 31

Speechable http://en.speechable.com

Phraselt http://phrase.it

Fotobabble http://www.fotobabble.com

Blabberize http://blabberize.com

Blabberize Tutorial https://www.youtube.com/watch?v=FEtUu1r8Pe4

Veterans History Project (Library of Congress) http://www.loc.gov/vets

Class Time Capsule http://www.eduplace.com/act/capsule.html

Time Capsule Ideas on Pinterest https://www.pinterest.com/chularubia22/time-capsule-ideas

In Mrs. Goldberg's Kitchen http://thejewniverse.com/2015/the-new-site-that-lets-you-snoop-around-an-old-polish-jewish-kitchen

Match the Selfie to the Shelfie http://www.hurstpierpointcollege.co.uk/libblog/competition-match-the-selfie-to-the-shelfie

Persona Project https://www.flickr.com/photos/jasontravis/sets/72157603258446753

What's in Your Bag? http://whatsinyourbag.com

Then/Now http://then-and-now-photos.tumblr.com

Make a Photo Quilt http://www.instructables.com/id/Make-a-photo-quilt

---

This "paper quilt" was created with the collage editing option on PicMonkey. "Wildflowers Collage." (Photo by the author, Creative Commons license, some rights reserved. Retrieved from http://flickr.com/photos/dmcordell/16801432742.)

Activity 10: What's Their Story?

Bloom's levels of cognitive learning: Analyze, Create

Antique stores frequently sell miscellaneous photos and postcards. Have students create a backstory for the people in these images: what is their name, career, family background, etc. Describe what is happening in the photograph and what might have occurred before or after what is shown. Vintage photos could also be used to practice arranging and tagging images. (See also Activity 8, Reading and Responding to Images.)

Activity 11: The Storytelling Game

Bloom's levels of cognitive learning: Analyze, Create

Creating collaborative story lines is an engaging verbal or written activity. Give this concept a visual spin by telling the tale in images. Start the story with an image selected by the teacher. Brainstorm possible plot twists, make a storyboard, and assign individual students or groups of students the task of finding an image that expresses the action in their particular frame of the story. When all of the images are collected, upload them to a slideshow or PowerPoint. Assess how well the story flows and whether the pictures follow the original plot or suggest different, perhaps unexpected, interpretations.

Variations

- Have one group of students prepare the slideshow. Their classmates will be challenged to write a narrative fitting the images.

- Make things a bit more random (and interesting). Start with the teacher-selected image and then assign a different student each day to select the next photo in the sequence. After everyone has had a turn, host a special "premiere" when students will finally get to see the completed story as a slideshow.

- Go outside the classroom walls: do the visual story as a round-robin with students in another school. One school will start things off with a story-starter photo, the collaborating group will add the next image, and so on until a predetermined number of photos has been reached. Vote on a title, then share the completed story as a collage or slideshow.

Vintage images can make wonderful visual writing prompts. "Old Photos." (Photo by the author, Creative Commons license, some rights reserved. Retrieved from http://flickr.com/photos/dmcordell/16801415271.)

Activity 12: Digital Storytelling Festival

Bloom's levels of cognitive learning: Apply, Analyze, Evaluate, Create

To honor School Library Month in April 2015, the American Association of School Librarians (AASL) held a Digital Storytelling Festival. Entries had to address the theme, "Your School Library: Where Learning Never Ends." AASL selected four tools from its Best Websites for Teaching and Learning lists that were to be used to create the stories:

- Pre-K–Grade 2: Participants will create a digital artifact using Storybird. This site allows users to make art-inspired books by selecting images from a database of illustrations. Although student authors cannot upload their own original images, this website provides a good introduction to how to plan and construct a story.

- Grades 3–5: Participants will create a digital artifact using FlipSnack. A flipbook is a digital magazine. Choose the "Create from Scratch" option to add "texts, images, videos, links, audio . . . and more." It is important for students to understand that "story" does not exclusively refer to works of fiction. By using a tool like FlipSnack, they can craft compelling narratives using a variety of information sources.

- Grades 6–8: Participants will create a 3D pop-up digital storybook using ZooBurst. ZooBurst offers a number of options for creating storybooks with Augmented (AR) capabilities. Students can use images provided by the site or customize by uploading their own photographs. "Speech" can be added in the form of chat bubbles. Readers who have a camera installed in their computer can also experience any ZooBurst book in AR: once a special code is printed out, the camera scans it. Pages then "jump up" into the room and the reader can interact with the book by the wave of a hand.

- Grades 9–12: Participants will create a digital video using Animoto. Animoto is a video creation service that assembles slideshows from photos. Music can be imported as well or chosen from the copyright-friendly playlist on the site. While editing options are limited, Animoto does create professional-looking products without requiring prior video production experience. If the first mix of photos and effects isn't acceptable, the site will do a remix without the necessity of uploading photos again.

Extension Activities

- Use FlipSnack to create a magazine about the school or community, illustrating the text with students' photographs. Embed a link to the FlipSnack on the school website or in the district newsletter. Have students present their work at a School Board meeting.

- Make a FlipSnack about Current Events for a social studies or journalism class project.

- Compile "Story of Me" ZooBurst books, with images of family members, favorite objects, etc., for Parents Night. Let student volunteers demonstrate how to use the AR option for a 3D viewing experience.

- Create a "Day in the Life" Animoto. Have students take a series of photos throughout the day, then use them in a short presentation.

Resource Box 32

AASL Digital Storytelling Festival http://www.ala.org/aasl/slm/2015/storytelling

AASL Best Websites for Teaching and Learning http://www.ala.org/aasl/standards-guidelines/best-websites

Storybird http://www.storybird.com

FlipSnack http://www.flipsnack.com

FlipSnack Create from Scratch http://www.flipsnack.com/blog/new-make-flipbooks-from-scratch-or-edit-your-pdfs

Zooburst http://www.zooburst.com

Animoto https://animoto.com

Assessment and Evaluation

"Perhaps more than in many other disciplines, study in the arts engages students in active learning focused on project-based demonstration of newly learned skills. In a visual arts classroom, students must routinely construct new knowledge based on the concepts, principles, and skills they are learning and apply it in practice in a studio situation. In art education, there is essentially no other way" (Eck, *Evaluation and Assessment in Middle-Level Art Education – Applications of Constructivist Theory*, p. 2).

"Assessing" is not synonymous with "grading." Quality assessment practices offer support to students at each step of the learning process. They create opportunities for students to display critical thinking skills by demonstrating the original products they have created. Both students and teachers can use information gained through various assessments to map future learning. Within the framework of identified goals and objectives, students should be encouraged to experiment, explore, and reflect upon what they have discovered. With the teacher serving as guide and consultant—providing feedback, encouragement, and constructive criticism—students are free to grow as learners.

There are a number of tools available for the review of digital photography projects, including rubrics, portfolios, checklists, and peer- and self-assessments:

- Buck Institute for Education (BIE Rubrics): Site includes rubrics for creativity and innovation, collaboration, and presentation, both CCSS-aligned

---

Resource Box 33

Buck Institute for Education (BIE) Rubrics http://bie.org/objects/cat/rubrics

Ms. Gray's Photo Rubric http://grayartclass.wordpress.com/photo-rubric **and How to Critique** http://grayartclass.wordpress.com/how-to-critique

New York State: Assessment in the Arts http://www.p12.nysed.gov/guides/arts/partIII1.pdf

Art 1 Final Exam http://theotherartone.blogspot.com.au

Yes, You Can Teach and Assess Creativity http://www.edutopia.org/blog/you-can-teach-assess-creativity-andrew-miller

Project Based Learning (PBL) Checklists http://www.educatorstechnology.com/2014/09/must-have-project-based-learning.html

Evaluating Student Presentations http://www.ncsu.edu/midlink/rub.pres.html

EPortfolio (Digital Portfolio) Rubric https://www2.uwstout.edu/content/profdev/rubrics/eportfoliorubric.html

"Portfolios: Assessment Across the Arts" http://artsedge.kennedy-center.org/educators/how-to/supporting-individual-needs/Portfolios-assessment-through-the-arts.aspx

Prince George's County Public Schools: Portfolio Assessment http://www1.pgcps.org/uploadedfiles/region_4_schools/high/gwynn_park/academics/family_and_consumer_science_files/portfolios-child_development-10.pdf

---

and non-CCSS, for grades K–12. Requires a free sign-up in order to download printable copies.

- Basic Photo Rubric from Ms. Gray's Art Classes: Her "How to Critique" page guides students in their evaluation of visual works of art.

- New York State Assessments in the Arts: This document-in-progress includes a variety of portfolio and assessment models.

- Art 1 Final Exam: These summative assessments require students to reflect upon their artwork and describe a companion presentation. This concept could easily be adapted for digital photography assignments.

- Project Based Learning (PBL) Checklists: Helpful for both formative and summative assessment of student projects and products.

- Evaluating Student Presentations: A rubric from the North Carolina Department of Public Instruction.

- EPortfolio (Digital Portfolio) Rubric: This rubric may be used for self-assessment and peer feedback as well as teacher assessment.

- "Portfolios: Assessment Across the Arts": An overview of portfolios, from the Kennedy Center.

- Prince George's County Public Schools: Criteria for building and assessing student portfolios.

Endnote: Why Photography Matters

"What we really long for, as human beings, is to be visible to each other."

—Jacqueline Novogratz

With increasingly tight budgets, and an emphasis on STEM (Science, Technology, Engineering, and Math) education, some people question whether the arts belong in schools.

The Rhode Island School of Design answered this query by recommending that STEAM (STEM + Art) be integrated into the K–20 curriculum, arguing that art and design complement the STEM disciplines and help nurture the creativity and innovation necessary for our future prosperity as a nation.

The arts, including photography, aren't "just" for school and career, however. In our increasingly visual society, photographs help us to define who we are, what we believe, and how we wish to live our lives. We capture and preserve what is important to us; each photo we snap becomes part of the digital legacy we leave behind. Images can communicate stories, our stories. They teach us to see ourselves and our world with fresh eyes.

"Could a greater miracle take place than for us to look through each other's eyes for an instant?"

—Henry David Thoreau

"Take and Leave." (Photo by the author, Creative Commons license, some rights reserved. Retrieved from http://flickr.com/photos/dmcordell/14489129962.)

Works Cited

American Academy of Pediatrics. "Children, Adolescents, and the Media." *Pediatrics* 132.5 (2013): 958–961. Web. 27 July 2014.

"Authentic Learning." *The Glossary of Education Reform*. Portland, ME: Great Schools Partnership, 2013. n. pag. Web. 5 Aug. 2014.

Bamford, Anne. *The Visual Literacy White Paper*. Adobe Systems Incorporated, 2003. Web. 25 May 2014.

Bronstein, M. J. *Photoplay!: Doodle. Design. Draw.* San Francisco: Chronicle Books, 2014. Print.

Brown, Nicole E., Kaila Bussert, Denise Hattwig, and Ann Medaille. "Keeping Up With . . . Visual Literacy." *Association of College & Research Libraries*. American Library Association, Oct. 2013. Web. 22 May 2014.

Churches, Andrew. "Bloom's Digital Taxonomy." *Educational Origami.* n. p. 2009. Web. 26 May 2014.

Debes, John L. "Some Foundations for Visual Literacy." *Audiovisual Instruction* 13 (1968): 961–64.

Declaration of Principles on Tolerance. Paris: UNESCO, 1995. Web. 26 May 2014.

Eck, Lorien R. "Evaluation and Assessment in Middle-Level Art Education—Applications of Constructivist Theory." *Journal for the Practical Application of Constructivist Theory in Education* 1.2 (2006). n. pag. Web. 25 Aug. 2014.

enGauge 21st Century Skills: Literacy in the Digital Age. North Central Regional Educational Laboratory and the Metiri Group, 2003. Web. 25 May 2014.

"English Language Arts Standards." *Common Core State Standards Initiative*. CoreStandards.org, 2014. Web. 5 Aug. 2014.

A Framework for Quality in Digital Media. Fred Rogers Center for Early Learning and Children's Media at Saint Vincent College, Apr. 2012. Web. 22 June 2014.

"Frequently Asked Questions." *Core Standards*. Common Core State Standards Initiative, 2014. Web. 24 May 2014.

Gardner, Howard. *The Unschooled Mind: How Children Think and How Schools Should Teach*. New York: Basic Books, 1991. Print.

Hattwig, Denise, Joanna Burgess, Kaila Bussert, and Ann Medaille. "ACRL Visual Literacy Competency Standards for Higher Education." American Library Association, October 2011. Web. 26 May 2014.

"ISTE Standards for Students." *ISTE Standards for Students*. International Society for Technology in Education, 2014. Web. 30 Sept. 2014.

Jimenez, L. M. "Sequencing Expert Readers' Metacognitive Strategies in Graphic Novels." Paper presented at the American Educational Research Association conference, Philadelphia, April 2014.

Just, Marcel. "Watching the Human Brain Process Information." Interview by Melissa Ludtke. *Nieman Reports*, 2010. Web. 25 May 2014.

McMains, Mary. "Vision & Learning." *VisionandLearning.org*. Makakumu Enterprises, 2008. Web. 26 May 2014.

Obama, President Barack. *Presidential Proclamation—National Day of Making, 2014*. Washington, DC: The White House. Office of the Press Secretary, 17 June 2014. Web. 19 Aug. 2014.

"Oxford Dictionaries Word of the Year 2013." Web blog post. *OxfordWords Blog*. Oxford University Press, 19 Nov. 2013. Web. 25 May 2014.

"P21 Common Core Toolkit." The Partnership for 21st Century Skills, 2011. Web. 26 May 2014.

Rideout, V. J. *Learning at Home: Families' Educational Media Use in America*. A Report of the Families and Media Project. New York: Joan Ganz Cooney Center at Sesame Workshop, 2014. Web. 13 Sept. 2015.

Riener, Cedar, and Daniel Willingham. "The Myth of Learning Styles." *Change: The Magazine of Higher Learning* 42.5 (2010): 32–35. Web. 22 May 2014.

Schulten, Katherine. "New Feature: What's Going On in This Picture?" Web blog post. *The Learning Network*. The New York Times Company, 15 Oct. 2012. Web. 26 May 2014.

Schwarz, Hunter. "How Many Photos Have Been Taken Ever?" *BuzzFeed.com*. BuzzFeed, Inc. 24 Sept. 2012. Web. 26 May 2014.

Standards for the 21st-Century Learner. Chicago: American Association of School Librarians, 2009. Print.

Takeuchi, Laurie, and Reed Stevens. *The New Coviewing: Designing for Learning Through Joint Media Engagement*. New York: Joan Ganz Cooney Center at Sesame Workshop and LIFE Center, 2011. Web. 26 May 2014.

Technology and Interactive Media as Tools in Early Childhood Programs Serving Children from Birth through Age 8. Joint Position Statement. National Association for the Education of Young Children and the Fred Rogers Center for Early Learning and Children's Media at Saint Vincent College, 2012. Web. 22 June 2014.

Thibault, Melissa, and David Walbert. "Reading Images: An Introduction to Visual Literacy." *Learning NC*. UNC School of Education, 2003. Web. 26 May 2014.

Thomas, Sue, Chris Joseph, Jess Laccetti, et al. "Transliteracy: Crossing Divides." *First Monday* 12.12 (2007). n.p. University of Illinois at Chicago. Web. 26 May 2014.

Velders, Teun, Sjoerd De Vries, and Loreta Vaicaityte. *Visual Literacy and Visual Communication for Global Education*. Enschede, Netherlands: University of Twente, 2007. Web. 26 May 2014.

"What Is 'Visual Literacy?'" *IVLA*. International Visual Literacy Association, 2012. Web. 26 May 2014.

Willingham, Daniel. "Learning Styles Don't Exist." *YouTube*. YouTube, 21 Aug. 2008. Web. 26 May 2014.

Index

About the Author

DIANE M. CORDELL is a retired K–12 teacher librarian who currently works as an education consultant and writer for CyberSmart Education Company. She contributed to the AASL White Paper "Educational Technology in Schools" as well as to *Embedded Librarianship: Tools and Practices* and *School Libraries: What's Now, What's Next, What's Yet to Come*. She also published "Create, Curate, Celebrate: Storytelling in the Library" in *Library Media Connection*. Cordell holds a master's degree in library science from Palmer School of Library and Information Science at Long Island University and a New York State Permanent Certification, School Media Specialist (Library).